W9-CLW-441

Praise for *The Emotionally Absent Mother*

"With compassion and sparkling clarity, Jasmin Lee Cori describes the effects of being undermothered and what it takes to overcome them. Her book will be of great value to new mothers serious about creating a loving environment for their children, adult sons and daughters who want at long last to fill the holes in their hearts, and clinicians interested in understanding and healing the mother wound."

—EVELYN BASSOFF, PHD, psychotherapist, author of *Mothers and Daughters: Loving and Letting Go*

"This book is a revelation to those of us whose mothering was short of what we needed. The author sensitively and authoritatively weaves developmental principles into a compassionate understanding of what it means to be undermothered."

—CONNIE DAWSON, PHD, coauthor of *Growing Up Again: Parenting Ourselves, Parenting Our Children*

"Jasmin Lee Cori has done a superb job of describing the importance of childhood attachment needs and the psychological wounds that get inflicted when an emotionally absent mother cannot meet those needs well enough. She has skillfully laid out clear steps wounded adults can take to identify their inner strengths and heal attachment wounds. I wholeheartedly recommend this book for anyone who wishes to understand and heal the wounds that can arise when parented by an emotionally absent mother."

—SHIRLEY JEAN SCHMIDT, MA, LPC, author of *The Developmental Needs Meeting Strategy: An Ego State Therapy for Healing Adults with Childhood Trauma and Attachment Wounds*

THE EXPERIMENT

BECAUSE EVERY BOOK IS A TEST OF NEW IDEAS

"With a compassionate and steady voice, Jasmin Lee Cori guides the reader through the difficult terrain faced by adults who have grown up without sufficient emotional mothering. Relying on personal experience and practice as a psychotherapist, she provides insight and tools to help readers overcome the challenges of a painful childhood and to move into the pleasures of living adult life fully."

— **KATHRYN BLACK, MA,** psychotherapist, author of *Mothering Without a Map: The Search for the Good Mother Within*

"This book effortlessly intertwines neuroscience with clinical acumen in a lovely work of extraordinary depth. In her compelling, heartrending analysis of the importance of motherhood, Jasmin Lee Cori has created a work as significant as Alice Miller's *Prisoners of Childhood*. Easily accessible and very useful, it is a must-read for parents-to-be, those in the helping professions, and adults who have been wounded by a negligent parent."

— **KATE CROWLEY, OTD, OTR/L,** Adjunct Faculty, University of Southern California, Specialist in Infant Mental Health

# THE EMOTIONALLY ABSENT MOTHER

Also by Jasmin Lee Cori, MS, LPC

*Healing from Trauma: A Survivor's Guide to Understanding Your Symptoms and Reclaiming Your Life*

*The Tao of Contemplation: Re-Sourcing the Inner Life*

*The Tarot of Transformation* (with Willow Arlenea)

# THE EMOTIONALLY ABSENT MOTHER

a guide to self-healing
and getting the love you missed

JASMIN LEE CORI, MS, LPC

**THE EXPERIMENT**

New York

THE EMOTIONALLY ABSENT MOTHER: *A Guide to Self-Healing and Getting the Love You Missed*

Copyright © Jasmin Lee Cori, 2010

All rights reserved. Except for brief passages quoted in newspaper, magazine, radio, television, or online reviews, no portion of this book may be reproduced, distributed, or transmitted in any form or by any means, electronic or mechanical, including photocopying, recording, or information storage or retrieval system, without the prior written permission of the publisher.

The Experiment, LLC
260 Fifth Avenue
New York, NY 10001-6408
www.theexperimentpublishing.com

The Experiment's books are available at special discounts when purchased in bulk for premiums and sales promotions as well as for fund-raising or educational use. For details, contact us at info@theexperimentpublishing.com.

Library of Congress Control Number: 2010924687

ISBN 978-1-61519-028-7
Ebook ISBN 978-1-61519-123-9

Cover design by Alison Forner
Cover photograph by Mark Barrett | Getty Images
Author photograph by Gail A. Bishop
Text design by Scott Harmon

Manufactured in the United States of America
Distributed by Workman Publishing Company, Inc.
Distributed simultaneously in Canada by Thomas Allen and Son Limited
First published August 2010
10 9 8

*To the motherless child*
*who somehow survived*
*all that was missing,*
*even when Mother was there.*
*This book is for you.*

## Mommy, Where Were You?

My first steps
I stood there teetering, so proud,
ecstatic as a baby bird learning it could fly.
When I looked back, my smile about to break my face,
I couldn't find you.
Mommy, where were you?

My first day of school
boarded onto that noisy, clackety bus
going to a strange place
kids crowding, adults peering,
the whole world new to me.
Mommy, where were you?

The first time I came home crying
the butt of children's laughter,
their words still stinging in my head,
I would have liked some consolation
but you were silent.

You are there in old photographs
but in my memories, you are missing.
I don't remember cuddling or being comforted
no special moments, just the two of us
I don't remember your smell or the feel of your touch.

I remember the color of your eyes
and the pain deep inside them
the pain usually hidden, like so much else,
beneath the mask I couldn't get behind.

You looked but didn't see me.
Your warmth never reached my little girl's heart.
Why did we miss each other, Mommy?
Where were you?
Was it because of me?

*– JC*

# Contents

# Introduction

Few experiences in life are as deep as the feelings we carry about our mothers. The roots of some of these feelings are lost in the dark recesses of preverbal experience. The branches go every which way, some holding glorious, sun-drenched moments, while others are broken off, leaving sharp and jagged edges that we get caught on. Mother is not a simple subject.

On both a cultural and a psychological level, our feelings about mothers are often inconsistent and tangled. Mom and apple pie are potent symbols, venerated in our national psyche but neglected in national policy, as reflected, for example, in our meager family leave policies in comparison with other developed countries. If we were really serious about mothering, we would provide more financial and in-home help as well as education for mothers. As it currently stands, mothers are held up on a pedestal with little support beneath them.

As adults we are aware of this. Few escape the feeling that mothers are to be honored, or the awareness that mothers are too often taken for granted, their sacrifices unappreciated. Yet many of us are secretly (or not so secretly) unsatisfied with what we got from our mothers, resentful that—whether their fault or not—they failed to provide important aspects of what we needed. And we're paying the price.

These are sensitive issues—sensitive for mothers and sensitive for all of us. Some, in a need to make mothers off-limits from criticism, become critical of those who are unsatisfied, blaming us for blaming our mothers, as if we are unfairly passing off the responsibility for our suffering. While I don't deny that some may use blame as a distraction and fail to take responsibility for the arduous task of healing, what I see more often as a therapist is the enormous guilt and resistance people have to work through to stop protecting their mothers. It is as if, even within the privacy of our own minds, we are afraid to criticize her. We are protecting the image of mother inside, protecting our fragile relationship with her by denying anything that might unsettle it, and protecting ourselves from the disappointment, anger, and pain that we've kept out of consciousness. As I will explain in the chapters that follow, many don't dare to uncover the painful truth of what was missing in their mothers because they are unprepared to deal with what this would mean.

Any relationship as complex as that between mother and child is going to include both love and hate. Most young children feel moments of hatred when their needs or wishes are frustrated, although many children wouldn't dare express this, their bond with Mommy far too fragile. And virtually all children feel love for Mother, even when that love is buried or walled off. As Robert Karen eloquently reported in his compilation of research on attachment:

> *Virtually all children, even abused children, love their parents. It's built into the nature of being a child. They may be hurt, disappointed, caught in destructive modes of being that ward off any possibility of getting the love they yearn for, but to be attached, even anxiously attached, is to be in love. Each year the love may become a little more difficult to access; each year the child may disavow his wish for connection more firmly; he may even swear off his parents and deny that he has any love for them at all; but the love is there, as is the longing to actively express it and to have it returned, hidden like a burning sun.[1]*

Karen's words show some of the complexity of this relationship. No one escapes wanting a mother's love.

Mothering is also a sensitive topic for those who are mothers. When I was first working on this book, I noticed some guilt and defensiveness when I would share with women who were mothers what I was writing about. They wanted to say, "Don't give me so much power. There are many other influences in a child's life. It's not all my fault how they turned out." All very true. We come in with individual differences that are often stunning. And there are other childhood influences as well, including birth order, bonding with and availability of Father and his adequacy as a parent, environmental and genetic influences on a child's basic physiology, family dynamics and important events in the family such as a major illness, and the stresses in the larger culture.

Despite these many factors, the impact of Mother is unparalleled. An attentive, capable, caring mother can help make up for many other handicaps, and the absence of such mothering is perhaps the greatest handicap of all, because when Mother is not doing her larger-than-life job as it needs to be done, children have significant deficits in their foundations.

My focus on the mother is not because mothers need more guilt or responsibility heaped on, but because the quality of the mothering we receive so powerfully shapes our development. My hope is that understanding these influences will lead us to better understand ourselves and, most important, to complete the developmental tasks and heal the injuries that resulted from insufficient mothering.

For those readers who are mothers or who are becoming mothers, it is my hope that my breaking down the roles of mothering as I do here and highlighting the central importance of nurturing will help train your focus. Although there are aspects of mothering that are instinctive and are passed through the generations by women who were well mothered themselves, for many good mothering must be consciously learned. If you were undermothered, your task will be twofold:

to heal your own wounds and to open up a different way of being with your children than your mother was with you.

Although a lack of good mothering affects men and women somewhat differently, there are also many common elements. Since there are a number of books about the gender-specific effects, I am looking at the aspects shared by both sexes. I am also focusing on a specific style of inadequate mothering related to the mother who is emotionally disengaged or "absent." There are many reasons she may be absent, and these will be detailed.

As I began working, I wanted to supplement my understanding of the undermothered adults I had experienced within my own circle and in my psychotherapy practice, so I put out a call for "undermothered" adults to interview. I was immediately flooded with responses. As might be expected, I found more women than men who were willing to talk with a stranger about their experiences, although I also had more access to women. There was nothing scientific about my sampling, so I can't claim to have captured the undermothered from a demographic or sociological perspective, but I think their brave and often insightful disclosures have some value for us all. Some of my findings are sprinkled throughout the chapters, but most of them are found in chapter 6, "Voices of the Undermothered," where I describe both the childhood environments my interviewees experienced and the challenges they have faced as adults.

Chapter 1 describes, in rather ideal terms, the role of mothering and introduces the term *Good Mother*. Chapter 2 dissects this further by talking about the various roles that the Good Mother plays in a child's life. This is followed by a chapter on attachment, which is a reflection of the strength and quality of the mother–child bond. The effects of secure attachment or insecure attachment follow us all the way into adult life. Chapter 4 includes other essential elements of good mothering, such as nurturing touch, relaxation, and safety.

From there we transition to what it is like when Mother is missing. Chapter 5 ("Mommy, Where Were You?") describes the emotionally absent mother, the reasons for her absence, and how this is experienced. This is augmented by the descriptions from the interviews included in chapter 6.

Our discussion of healing begins in chapter 7 with an overview of the healing process. Chapter 8 focuses on psychotherapy as a container for this healing, with all the following chapters more about self-help. Chapter 9 is about connecting with "Good Mother energy," whether in archetypal form or in the person of helpful others, including mates. The theme of being re-parented is amplified in chapter 10, where the focus is on inner child work and becoming your own best mother. Chapter 11 takes a more current-day, proactive approach by looking at developmental needs that were not met earlier and talking about practical strategies for meeting them now. The final chapter, chapter 12, helps you get a more objective picture of your mother and examine the dance between the two of you. It addresses the issues of undermothered adults' current relationships with Mom, how we change the family legacy with our own children, and what we can reasonably expect in terms of healing.

There are a number of exercises in the book, which you are free to complete or not. There are also pauses throughout the book that invite you to digest the material and reflect on your own situation. I encourage you to take a moment to consider these, listening for what comes to mind as you read them, even if you don't choose to formally answer each question. Since what you take away for yourself in terms of your own understanding and healing is an important benefit to reading this book, I invite you to take your time. You have to be your own gatekeeper here, so if working with particular material is distressing, consider what kind of support you need and what is too much stimulation for you in any given moment. Practice being a good mother to yourself by taking on only what you can handle at any given moment. You can always come back to the material at another time.

It may help to have support from other readers who are working with this material. To that end, I have set up an online support group. (See p. 212 for more information.)

My three goals in this book are:

🌱 To help you assess in what ways and to what extent you were undermothered.

🌱 To help you see the connection between the mothering you experienced and the difficulties in your life. What have been thought of as personal *defects* can then be linked to mothering *deficits*, relieving self-blame.

🌱 To provide suggestions for how these missing elements can be made up for now—whether in therapy, through close relationships, or by providing them for yourself.

The good news is that the deficits of inadequate mothering can be made up for later—maybe not completely, but more significantly than we usually dare to hope. We can heal the unloved child and become empowered, loving adults. This is a journey worth taking.

# 1.

# Mothering

## Mother as the tree of life

I will always remember an image in *The Family of Man,* a photo exhibit that traveled the world and was captured in book form. A tall, lanky black woman stood with two young children, their faces dark, caught in shadow.* On the facing page, quoting Proverbs, were these words: *She is a tree of life to them.*

A tree of life. A tree providing shelter, home, protection. A tree you can climb on and eat from. A tree that seems big when you are many times smaller. A tree that is *your* tree.

In world mystical traditions, the tree of life is the vertical axis around which life revolves. In a similar way, Mother is the axis around which the family and the child's emotional life revolve. In the vast stretch of history before the Christian era, the tree of life was often depicted as a mother, and the Great Mother/Goddess was often depicted as a tree.

Thus the tree is a natural symbol for mothering. With its fruits and flowers, with birds and animals in and around it, it provides both shelter and supply. Growing in many directions, but particularly with its arc of outward expansion, it is like a fountain of abundance. Part of the tree-of-life archetype is this sense of bounty and of giving.

This archetype is captured in the children's book *The Giving Tree* by Shel Silverstein. Originally published in 1964, it is

* The photograph was taken by Consuelo Kanaga.

considered a classic parable of love and devotion. It is about a boy and a tree that loves him very much and gives him everything she has. She lets him swing on her branches, gives him shade to sit under, apples to eat, and branches to build a house. She even lets him cut down her trunk to make a boat. In the end, the tree only a stump and the boy an old man, she gives him a place to rest.

As many have clearly noted, the relationship between the boy and tree is much like that between a child and mother. The tree puts the boy's needs first. It gives and gives and gives. This is part of the role of a mother, which competes at times with a woman's own needs to develop herself as a person apart from her mothering role and her relationship with others. Many women have lamented losing themselves in mothering and in being partners. Yet if a woman isn't ready, at least for a period of her life, to attend to the needs of others, she really isn't ready for the task of mothering.

There are many legitimate reasons a woman may be unable to fully take on the enormous task of mothering, yet unfortunately women have often not been given (or not felt) a choice about this. Because of either unintentional pregnancy or social expectations, women may slide into motherhood without really choosing it. Often such women have not yet grown into full adults themselves. They are ill equipped for what lies in front of them.

It is not easy to give of yourself if you still have many unmet needs. Yet mothering requires constant giving. A good mother shares the warmth of her body when her child is cold, the milk from her breast when her child needs nourishment. She **gives** both the unborn child and the nursing child calcium from her bones. This is a very basic level of giving of oneself. No wonder "Mother" is a symbol of sacrifice!

## Mommy is what we are made of

There are two important levels to the assertion that we are made of our mothers. The first is the obvious biological fact: We were made in her body, and we are made from her body. Then there is the psychological level where Mother is part of our personality, psyche, and structure. It's as if she is literally a layer of our being. You'll get a better understanding of this in the next several chapters.

How we are put together, how we see ourselves, our sense of self-esteem, our unconscious beliefs about relationship—all of these are strongly imprinted by our mother. She is not the only influence, but she and our interactions with her provide the basic building materials for all of these things.

Whether we feel that basic material as nourishing or toxic is largely determined by the quality of our interactions with our mother. It is not what Mother *does* that is so critical, but rather her energetic presence and her love that are so important. Is she spaced out or angry while feeding her baby? When Mother is really there in a loving way, then Mommy's milk and Mommy's heart don't feel separate. When she's not there, her milk is not as sustaining. The baby may feel not quite right taking it, perhaps because it is not so freely given or because there's something unwanted in the interaction that comes along with the milk.

As they would say in a children's book, when this interaction is good, it feels very, very good, and when it is bad, it feels horrid. Of course this view is more black and white than things usually are, but young children experience the world with great intensity. You can feel Mother as an inner layer of support, of love that is always with you, or you can feel as if there is something dead or toxic in you. This toxic substance is what you absorbed from your interactions with her and perhaps from what was toxic inside her.

## Who can mother?

I use the term *mother* all through the book, yet I don't necessarily limit this to the woman who gives birth to a particular child—although that relationship, even if it never goes beyond birth (because the mother dies or gives the baby away), marks a person's entire life. When I ask about your mother in this book, I'm asking about the person who functioned in this primary role, and the term *Good Mother* can refer to any adult who takes on a caring, nurturing, protective role in your life, fulfilling the functions described in the next chapter.

This can include an adoptive mother, grandmother, or stepmother; even the right father can fill these shoes. Others further outside the inner family circle can help meet some of the needs (even into adulthood): teachers, aunts, mothers of friends, therapists, partners. We can even meet some of these needs for ourselves as we mature, understanding that the undermothered child is usually still alive in an adult, still needing what it needed then.

Although not every woman adapts to the role of mothering, nature has done its best to give biological mothers every advantage. Research supports the idea that mothers, as a group, instinctively employ behaviors that infants prefer. Studies in Sweden found that even when a mother works outside the home and the father is the primary caretaker, babies still strongly prefer being with the mother.[2]

Nature also supports biological mothers through their hormones (especially oxytocin), which seem to put them in the mood for bonding and are directly correlated with bonding behaviors. Breast-feeding puts the infant at the perfect distance at which it can focus on the mother's eyes. Of course the developing fetus has already been forming a relationship with the mother in the womb, responding to her heartbeat, her voice, her touch through the abdominal wall, and her energetic presence. Yet these biological advantages aren't enough for some women to overcome the lack of readiness they show for taking on the tasks of mothering. It is a good thing, then, that people other than biological mothers can "mother."

## The good-enough mother

Mothers don't need to be perfect, and can't be. The perfection, when there, is supplied through the eyes of the child—who, when the mother does a good-enough job meeting his or her basic needs, feels total adoration. This is helpful, because when you're totally dependent on someone, you want to believe that person can do the job. To overlook the slips and lack of perfect attunement and accentuate the positive is both good psychological strategy and good evolutionary strategy, since the child's good feelings also help the mother bond to the child.

The term *good-enough mother* was coined by the famous pediatrician and psychoanalyst D. W. Winnicott to describe the mother who provides enough for a child to have a good start in life. Winnicott sees the primary job of the good-enough mother as adapting to the baby. He describes how the good-enough mother starts off with almost complete adaptation to her infant's needs, and then adapts less and less as the infant can tolerate more frustration. A mother who continued to satisfy all the infant's needs perfectly and immediately would rob the baby of the need to learn new behaviors, develop new skills, and be able to handle delay and frustration.

Recent research reinforces this notion that the mother doesn't have to be 100 percent attuned and available to her child to offer good-enough parenting. It suggests that what is needed is to be in sync (defined as in a harmonious state together, with the mother attuned to the child) 30 percent of the time.[3] Is that really so much to ask?

According to psychotherapist and author Diana Fosha, "What matters as much as (if not more than) the natural capacity to be in sync is the capacity to repair out-of-syncness so as to reestablish optimal connection."[4] The good-enough mother needs to repair the inevitable ruptures that occur in every relationship. She is not going to always behave just right, but she has to know how to make it right when she misses.

Research suggests that she has help in this from her child. Babies come into the world with an urge toward and capacity for maintaining a strong bond with their mothers. They are also wired to make the most of the mother's reparative efforts.[5] For a child to be able to rectify the inevitable disruptions in this relationship is empowering, as you can imagine. Conversely, to not be able to get Mother's attention, to not be able to reconnect after there has been a disconnection, can leave the baby feeling profoundly impotent and discouraged about relationships and about getting her needs met.

When the mother is checked out and not attuned enough to respond to the child's needs, the child ends up adapting to the mother instead of the other way around. Losing touch with his core experience, the child then develops what Winnicott calls a *false self.*

### Good Mother messages

How Mother responds to our basic needs tells us about our importance to her. Is she generous in giving to us (even joyful!), or does she meet our needs with a sense of burden and an attitude that says, *"You're bothering me"*? When she changes a diaper or dresses us, is her touch gentle and loving, or is it efficient and slightly brusque? Perhaps it seems mechanical. What do her eyes say? How about the expressions on her face? What do her actions and choices convey? All of these are a part of a mother's communication and shape our relationship to her. Together they form the basis of the messages we receive.

We can start by looking at what may be called "Good Mother messages"[6] and then consider what those of us who are undermothered heard instead.

Here are ten basic Good Mother messages:

- 🍃 I'm glad that you're here.

- 🍃 I see you.

- 🍃 You are special to me.

- 🍃 I respect you.

- 🍃 I love you.

- 🍃 Your needs are important to me. You can turn to me for help.

- 🍃 I am here for you. I'll make time for you.

- 🍃 I'll keep you safe.

- 🍃 You can rest in me.

- 🍃 I enjoy you. You brighten my heart.

Let's look at these in more detail:

### I'm glad that you're here.

"I'm glad that you're here" is an important first message for a child to hear. This message is communicated through behaviors that tell the child she is valued and wanted.

Many believe that this fundamental sense of being wanted begins in utero. Certainly there are many moments in children's lives in which they feel either wanted or not. I would suggest that this is not an all-or-nothing experience but rather a matter of degree and that isolated moments of feeling unwanted can be counterbalanced to a great extent by a larger stream of experiences where the child feels valued.

The message "I'm glad you're here" helps *us* be glad that we're here. It helps us feel comfortable taking up space and being in our bodies.

### I see you.

A mother conveys "I see you" primarily through accurate mirroring (see Mother as Mirror, p. 31) and attuned responsiveness. She knows, for instance, what we like and what we don't. She knows what our interests are and how we feel about things. Being seen is being known.

### You are special to me.

The message "You are special to me" (usually not said in words) tells us that we are valued and prized. As is true with other messages, this needs to be paired with the sense of being seen for who we are so that we do not associate specialness with some superficial, external quality or image.

### I respect you.

A mother communicates "I respect you" when she supports a child's uniqueness, doesn't try to control when there is no need to, accepts the child's preferences and decisions, and communicates that she values what she sees in the child. Children who feel respected and loved in a genuine way will have permission to discover and express their unique self rather than mirror the parent(s) or conform to some parental blueprint.

### I love you.

"I love you" is often conveyed by these simple words yet needs to be experienced as sincere and authentic in order to have meaning. Many children hear these words several times a day; others go a lifetime without them. It is important that they not be perceived as manipulative and not paired with requiring something of the child.

Love is probably most effectively communicated by nonverbal means, including touch, tone of voice, eyes and facial expression, body language, and attentiveness. When the environment provides a secure sense of holding and containment (such as provided through boundaries and rules), this also feels like love.

### Your needs are important to me. You can turn to me for help.

"Your needs are important to me" expresses a sense of priority. It's not just that Mother is saying, "I'll take care of you because I have to" or "when I get to it," but "because this is actually important." With this message, we get the sense that Mother's attentiveness comes out of love and genuine caring. "You can turn to me for help" gives permission; it says you don't have to hide your needs or try to take care of them yourself.

### I am here for you. I'll make time for you.

"I am here for you" is a way of saying, "You can count on me. I'm not going to disappear on you." Often this will relate to specific needs, but beyond that, it means "I am here as a consistent presence in your life." This supports a sense of relaxation and trust.

A related message would be "I'll make time for you." It expresses availability, priority, and valuing. Unfortunately, too many children feel that their parents don't have time for them.

### I'll keep you safe.

"I'll keep you safe" could also be expressed as "I'll protect you. I won't let you be hurt or overwhelmed (unnecessarily)."

A sense of safety is essential for a child to be able to relax and explore. Without safety, we may never learn to really go out into the world. Without our caretaker's protection, our only protection is to stay small and build defensive structures into our personality.

### You can rest in me.

"You can rest in me" is a way of saying several things. First, it implies a protected space; if you have to be on guard, you can't really rest. It also implies availability (Mother needs to be here to rest in) and acceptance. It is a way of saying, "With me, you can be at home." We all want a place where we can be totally ourselves, where we don't have to perform, and where we feel soothed and comforted in the company of another.

*I enjoy you. You brighten my heart.*

"I enjoy you" is an affirmation of the child's preciousness. We want not only to be respected but also to know that others take pleasure in our very being. The message "You brighten my heart" supports the child's presence and inner light. It helps build a sense of value and confidence.

## What happens when Good Mother messages are absent?

When these Good Mother messages are absent, they leave specific "holes" or feelings of deficiency. Using the above list, it might look like this:

*I'm glad that you're here.*

When we don't feel welcomed or wanted, we may conclude, "Maybe it would be better if I weren't here." It can also lead to a great fear of abandonment. One woman who never felt wanted as a child was terrified every time she went to a restaurant or Laundromat with her mother that her mother would leave her and never come back. For a young child to not feel wanted is to have no solid ground.

*I see you.*

If Mother doesn't see or know us, then her responses will not feel on target. She may try to guide, for instance, but starts in the wrong place.

When we are consistently not seen, it can lead to feeling invisible and an uncertainty that we are real. The feeling of un-reality can be subtle and generally unconscious, or it can be quite pervasive and disorienting.

*You are special to me.*

When we don't feel special to our parents, we don't feel cherished for who we are. We may even think, Mommy might like it better if I were someone else.

*I respect you.*

When we don't feel that our capacities, boundaries, and preferences are respected, we don't learn to respect these for ourselves. We may develop a sense of unworthiness and shame or fail to actualize our true potential. This can also set us up to be too accommodating to other people rather than stand behind ourselves.

*I love you.*

With an absence of sufficient loving, we may conclude, "I am unlovable as I am." Consequently, we may contort ourselves in the hope that "If I conform to what others want, maybe they'll love me."

*Your needs are important to me. I am here for you.*

When we don't get a sense that Mother wants to meet our needs, we can believe, "My needs are shameful or a burden. I shouldn't have needs." We feel alone in our experience.

*I'll keep you safe.*

Without the sense of protection, we can feel overwhelmed by life and conclude that the world is dangerous.

*You can rest in me.*

When being with Mother is not a safe place to be ourselves, we miss an important aspect of connection. Being with Mother then becomes a time we need to stay alert or perform, and we never fully feel at home with her.

*I enjoy you. You brighten my heart.*

Without a sense that Mother likes and actually enjoys us, we can conclude, "I am a burden that nobody wants. I wish I could disappear. I shouldn't take up so much space."

**The messages you received**

> Go through each of the ten Good Mother messages, and for each one note your emotional response to it. Does this message feel familiar? (Remember these messages are communicated by behaviors more than through words.) Is this a message you think you received? How does it feel in your body?

> You might compare each message in the first list with the corresponding one in the second list and see which seems more true for you, paying attention as best as you can to thoughts, emotions, and sensations in your body.

As with any exercise in this book, this may bring up uncomfortable feelings, so you'll want to pace yourself. If you find yourself feeling overwhelmed, you might let it go for now and come back to it when you are ready, or do the exercise when you have a supportive person present.

## What does it mean to be undermothered?

When you don't get enough good mothering, in terms of these Good Mother messages, the functions described in chapter 2, the secure attachment of chapter 3, or the nurturing touch and love and other building blocks in chapter 4, you are undermothered. Yes, you got enough mothering to survive, but not enough for the kind of foundation that supports healthy self-confidence, initiative, resilience, trust, healthy entitlement, self-esteem, and the many other qualities we need to thrive in this challenging world.

This book is not about "bad mothers" and their sins of commission (such as intrusive and abusive behaviors), but rather about their sins of omission—their failure to provide what the Good Mother provides. These sins of omission are found more often in mothers who can be described as disengaged, emotionally absent, or emotionally detached, terms that can be used interchangeably. Such mothers fail, in particular, to provide the emotional nourishment a child needs in order to develop, leaving a definite nurturing deficit.

Mothers who are often physically absent and/or exhausted and who are severely overstretched when at home may also contribute to this syndrome. This is not to suggest that mothers shouldn't work or have other important aspects of their lives, but mothers need to be energetically engaged with their children and attentive to their needs enough of the time that children can develop in healthy ways.

Although the severity of neglect and the coldness displayed by these mothers is often nothing short of astonishing, it's hard to blame these mothers when you see them more clearly. These are women who are depressed, dissociated, exhausted, stressed—the tree of life withered, now home to no one.

# 2.

# The Many Faces of the Good Mother

The perceptual world (and specifically the visual world) of the infant contains many experiences of the same few objects, yet each experience is quite distinct and different—so much so that, from the infant's point of view, they seem to be different objects. In a somewhat similar way, we can take the image of the Good Mother and separate it into different experiences, which I call the many faces of the Good Mother. Each "face" represents a role that she fulfills or a psychological function important for the child's development.

After reading this chapter, you may wonder how one person can fulfill so many important and seemingly endless tasks. Of course no one can perfectly, which makes our picture of the Good Mother an ideal or model. By reflecting on how well your mother fulfilled each of these psychological functions, you will understand more about her fingerprint on your psyche and bring more insight into your feelings, beliefs, and behaviors. You'll understand why some parts of you need more shoring up than others.

You'll also notice that many of these roles overlap, and it may seem arbitrary at moments to try to separate them. They work together to do their magic and create the larger-than-life archetype of the Good Mother. In dissecting the Good Mother this way, we may take away a little of her mystery, but perhaps the cost is worth it if it helps us see our needs more clearly and get serious about meeting them.

Please keep in mind that although I am talking about these as functions of the mother, they can be fulfilled by any caregiver and are not strictly limited to biological mothers. Fathers, grandparents, nannies, day care workers, extended family members, and even mother figures found later in life can provide some of these important nutrients.

The ten faces are as follows:

- Mother as *source*
- Mother as *place of attachment*
- Mother as *first responder*
- Mother as *modulator*
- Mother as *nurturer*
- Mother as *mirror*
- Mother as *cheerleader*
- Mother as *mentor*
- Mother as *protector*
- Mother as *home base*

## Mother as Source

"Mother" is what we come from and what we are made of. In mythology and religion, this source is often depicted as some kind of mother goddess, often an ocean goddess. Just as life is thought to have evolved from the ocean, human life evolves from the mother and, more specifically, the womb. Thus, at both the mythological level and the more mundane, the source of life is Mother.

When the child has a positive experience of Mother, he gets the sense "I am *of* Mommy. I come from her. I'm part of her. I'm like her." This becomes a building block of identity.

Unfortunately, not everyone has an experience of Mother as Source in a positive way. Some adults, through an experience of age regression in hypnosis or any kind of depth work, recover memories of the womb as a toxic environment they are trapped in. They have a strong sense of being "of"—but it's an icky "*of*" from which they would rather be separate. This also happens with engulfing mothers, who are not experienced in a positive way.

Then there is the experience of children put up for adoption whose source has, at least on a subjective level, rejected them. They are in the complex situation of both being "*of*" this first mother since she gave birth to them, and also "not *of*" her, because they do not continue to belong to her. Sometimes it's challenging for them to develop a firm sense of belonging to their adopted mother.

Having a sense of belonging somewhere is essential, and the sense of Mother as Source is only one part of it. As we'll see, it also comes into play when we experience Mother as the Place of Attachment.

Although some of this may be beyond Mother's control, there are things Mother can do to be experienced as source in a positive way. She can create a welcoming environment, from the first moments of life. She can be a positive energy that her children want to be around and are nourished by. She can draw similarities between herself and her child, while careful to give the child plenty of room to also be different. And she can be a positive role model that her children, throughout their lives, will be proud of.

**Your mother as source**

➤ When you think of your mother's womb, does it feel like an inviting place? If you can't imagine this, ask how it would feel to be enveloped in your mother's energy. Is that something you would like?

➤ Did you want to be like your mother or did you want to be as different as possible (or anything in between)? If someone said, "You are so like your mother!" how would you feel?

➤ Can you imagine feeling pride about being your mother's child, in being her offspring? Do you identify yourself in relation to your mother?

## Mother as Place of Attachment

Mother is our first connection to the world. Here we focus not on Mother as the ocean we come from, but as the more immediate place where we are attached, like the underside of a boat that a barnacle fastens to. Mother is the belly of the ship that a securely attached child clings to.

When you watch securely attached toddlers and young children with their mothers, they are in constant physical contact, climbing over, pulling on, sucking, and hugging the mother's body. Even an older child will take Mother's hand when scared. As we'll learn below, attachment is not created just through body contact but also through the mother's attunement and responsiveness to needs. Attachment is so important that the whole next chapter is devoted to it.

Attachment for the young child brings the feeling "I belong to you. And because I belong to you, I have a place." Without this, we are untethered, adrift well into our adult years. One woman felt like a piece of driftwood out at sea; another was so unbonded to her mother that she felt as if she must have been found under a cabbage leaf—or may as well have been. This can result in a profound sense of aloneness, alienation, and not belonging.

With secure attachment, a child feels securely held, safe. This function overlaps with Mother as First Responder because it is largely through this function of being responsive to needs that attachment is formed.

---

**Your mother as place of attachment**

➤ On a scale of 1 through 10 (with 10 being extremely connected), how connected would you say you feel to your mother? How has this changed throughout your life?

➤ What are your early memories around physical contact with your mother? Was she your jungle gym or was there more a sense of "Keep Out"?

➤ As a child, did you clearly feel part of your family? Did you feel bonded or adrift?

➤ Have you had feelings of being an orphan or motherless child?

## Mother as First Responder

A very important role that secures Mother in her role as place of attachment is what I call Mother as First Responder. The "first responders" in our modern world are firefighters and police officers, the folks you call when there is an emergency. Imagine your home is on fire and no one comes. How would that affect you in terms of believing help will be there when you need it?

As many authors have convincingly shown, every need feels urgent to a baby, and thus is an emergency. As babies, we had no way of meeting our basic needs and were entirely dependent on others to be responsive to our calls for help. When our needs are consistently met, we feel secure and trust that help will be there. Without this, we learn that care is not available, the world doesn't feel friendly or supportive, and we feel more insecure and mistrustful. We don't know that we will have what we need, which jeopardizes our basic sense of trust.

The Good Mother messages related to this are "I'll take care of you. Your needs are important to me. I am here for you. You can rest in me."

Of course, to do this, a mother needs to be tuned in to her child in an accurate way. It doesn't help if the first responder goes to the wrong address, offers shelter when what's needed is food, or insists on giving you what you don't want. In psychological parlance we call this accuracy "attunement." Mother as First Responder will be helpful to the extent she is attuned to her child's needs. This is especially true for the early years before language.

This attunement and responsiveness to needs provides what is called a holding environment. With it, we feel held. This function is also what leads to *self-regulation* (described next in Mother as Modulator).

**Your mother as first responder**

➤ It may be hard to remember how your mother responded to you as an infant and small child, but often a telltale clue is how you feel about your needs now. Are you respectful and attentive to your needs, or so ashamed of needing that you try to hide them? Or perhaps you are demanding. How you respond to your own needs most often parallels how your mother responded to your needs, unless there have been a number of significant imprinting experiences that gave you a different reference point.

➤ What information do you have about how your mother responded to your needs? What stories have you heard? What do photographs show?

➤ Beyond your early childhood, what do you know about how your mother tended to respond to other people's needs? Was she Johnny-on-the-spot? Resentful? Not so competent? Gracious? Did people need to ask multiple times? Did she meet what she assumed to be others' needs rather than finding out what the real needs were?

## Mother as Modulator

Mother as Modulator is very much interrelated with Mother as First Responder, but by tilting the picture just a little bit and giving it a different name, we see it in a different way.

When Mother is there as first responder, the fire doesn't rage out of control. To give but one example, the baby's hunger is met, and he can return to a state of homeostasis and rest. Imagine the intolerable discomfort when this is not true.

To *modulate* something is to make sure it's not too strong and not too weak, but falls within a more optimal range. The mother helps manage her child's physiological states, such as being hungry or cold, by meeting the child's needs so that he is not howling with discomfort, by soothing the child when he is distressed, and by helping the child hold his many feelings. Through her response, she teaches the child how to deal with disappointment, frustration, anger, loss, and the many powerful experiences of life.

Without Mother as an effective modulator, we don't learn to effectively manage our emotions. Either we cut off feelings, or our emotional states tend to spiral out of control. Anger turns into rage, crying to hysteria; we can't contain our excitement, frustration, sexual impulses, or anything else.

Learning to modulate our internal states is called *self-regulation* or *self-modulation*. It is something the nervous system for the most part controls, but it is learned initially by the mother standing in for the developing nervous system and by meeting the child's needs before he gets totally overwhelmed. Mother as Modulator serves as a cushion to the child's fragile nervous system while it is developing.

There are a number of ways a mother can accomplish this. She can soothe the distressed child (whether through touch, words, or simply her caring presence), help the child identify needs and emotions, help turn the child's attention away from the distress, thus modulating it, and provide reassurance. One woman who has suffered lifelong anxiety told me that she never once heard her mother say, "It will be all right." Her mother never calmed her or helped her feel better.

When Mother is modulator, she helps us transition from negative emotional experiences to positive ones. One way she does this is by first empathizing with what is going on, and then leading us to more comfortable territory. She shows us how to let go of one emotion and move on to another, and in her own cheerfulness gives us something brighter to join with. We see this in the mother who meets her child's tears with a sad face and soon has her child laughing.

On a yet more subtle level, Mother modulates a child's distress through a process more recently called *limbic resonance* or *limbic regulation*. In limbic regulation, one person's emotional brain entrains another's, whose emotional brain shifts to match the first person's. All mammals have this capacity, and it is thought to be a major mechanism through which an infant or young child's inner state is directly modulated by Mother. Just by gazing into the child's eyes, the mother communicates brain to brain with her child, bringing the child's limbic system into coherence with hers. (This is helpful when Mother is in a positive, regulated state but not when she is fussy and upset herself.)

An inability to regulate physiological arousal is common to trauma disorders like post-traumatic stress disorder (PTSD). When people lacking modulation are triggered by something, they can get so upset that they can't think clearly or stay fully present. It's as if there isn't a regulator on their system, so they can't keep their physical and emotional responses within a manageable or optimal range. Although we can learn self-regulation later in life, it saves us a lot of grief if Mother helps us master this critical skill early.

**Your mother as modulator**

➤ What do you know about how your mother responded to your needs in infancy? How available was she? How many other children was she also caring for? How attentive was she? Was she depressed or absorbed elsewhere?

➤ What philosophies shaped her parenting? Was she influenced by the school of thought that told parents to let their babies "cry it out"?

➤ Do you remember times when your mother provided reassurance or comfort when you were in distress? Did she help you through the hard times?

➤ Is your mother (or was she) good at regulating her own physiological needs—attending to hunger, thirst, need for sleep, or contact, for instance? Can she regulate her own emotions, keeping them in a moderate range while still truly feeling them?

➤ Was your mother good at tuning in to your emotional states? Did she seem to care about them? Did she teach you how to constructively manage emotions without simply suppressing them? Did she model healthy expression of emotions?

## Mother as Nurturer

We all recognize Mother in this role. An essential aspect of the archetype of the Good Mother is to be nurturing. Mother is nurturer on both physical and emotional levels, providing both physical and emotional nourishment. Often these are experienced together, as in breast-feeding. A mother feeds her baby her body and her love. Both are necessary for the baby to survive and to thrive.

Children seem to have an inherent ability to know when emotional nourishment is genuine (it truly does feed them) and when it's fake. A mother can profess to be very loving and involved with her child, and she can gain considerable recognition from the world for this, but the child will feel a hole in his soul when Mommy's love isn't genuine. It doesn't matter how many pronouncements Mother makes or how impeccable she is about physical care, if there isn't a sense of real contact and caring, the child will not experience Mother as a source of nurturance.

Since a child's first language is touch, much will be communicated by the mother's holding and handling of the infant as well as the way she continues to touch her growing child. Does the touch communicate real caring and love, or is it simply accomplishing the task at hand?

The main message associated with this function is "I love you." This is crucial to the development of self-esteem. When it is present, the child thinks, *Mommy loves me, so I am somebody.*

**Your mother as nurturer**

➤ As a child, did you feel loved by your mother? What memories support this?

➤ What do you as an adult know about this? Perhaps you recognize that she did love you but was severely limited in being able to express it, or that she was unable to love. Or perhaps you see that you were unable to let it in.

➤ On a scale of 1 through 10 (with 10 being extremely nurturing), where would you place your mother in terms of being nurturing? How has she nurtured others?

## Mother as Mirror

A mother's role in providing reflection is one of her most important. It is how children feel known and come to know themselves.

Mirroring happens both verbally and nonverbally, and there are several levels to it. The first is one where children feel contacted, met. When a child feels seen, she can recognize herself as a developing person. If the child feels invisible or not seen, often that child will feel not fully real. So the most fundamental message of mirroring is "I see you—and you are real."

Psychologists and others who study human development report that those qualities that are recognized in a child develop, whereas those that aren't often wither away. Think of the way children learn language: As linguists have noted, children start out making sounds from many, many languages, but only those sounds that are part of the parents' language are reinforced, and the other sounds fall out of the child's vocabulary. Similarly, emotions that are not seen, behaviors that are not seen, qualities that are not seen or not supported either fail to develop or go underground.

Verbal mirroring involves saying things like "You're really angry!" or "You're sad right now." Verbal mirroring helps a young child identify feelings and helps people of all ages feel heard. The process isn't limited to feelings; qualities are mirrored as well. "You're a pretty girl" and "My, aren't you smart!" are other examples.

Before the child develops language, mirroring is much more physical. It involves replicating the child's expressions: laughing when the child laughs, frowning when the child frowns, and so on. Because the baby can't reflect on or sense herself at this early stage, she needs a mirror to see herself.

The basic message of "I see you" is modified by the tone involved. It can be "I see you, and you are good" or "I see you, and you are bad." The first we might call the admiring mirror; the second could be considered a shaming mirror. An admiring mirror helps us stand tall, feel proud of ourselves, feel that we have a right to be here and it's good that we're here. Our sense of value derives greatly from this positive mirroring. The admiring mirror (when sincere and realistic) helps us develop self-respect.

In order for us to really feel seen, mirroring needs to be accurate. Distorted mirroring can have several results. One is conforming to what others believe about you, whether the message is that you're a slow learner or a troublemaker. In addition, distorted mirroring can lead to an ongoing attempt to get accurate mirroring. Some children and adults get aggravated when not seen accurately and try very hard to be understood. Others give up and feel invisible. Admiration, powerful as it is, paired with distorted mirroring doesn't hit the target and therefore doesn't do any good.

A further refinement of Mother as Mirror is when Mother acts as a compass. In this role, Mother knows you so well that she calls you on it when you are not being true to yourself, essentially saying, "That's not really you." As children, we try on many different costumes as we're coming to know ourselves, and having someone who knows us so well that she can (at the right time) say, "That doesn't quite fit you, darling," can be helpful. I use the word *compass* because in this role, Mother reflects to us when we're getting off course and seems to know what "true north" is to us.

Mirroring is so important that a lack of mirroring often leads to a lifelong craving for it.

---

**Your mother as mirror**

➤ Do you feel that your mother saw the real you? What gives you this impression?

➤ What nonverbal expressions, if any, stand out in your memory of your mother's response to you? (Tone of voice is also included in this category.) What did these communicate?

➤ Was she good at verbally reflecting back your states? If not, any ideas about why not?

➤ What are some aspects that she was best at mirroring, and what aspects did she miss? (For instance, she may have acknowledged your intelligence but not your feelings.)

➤ Did your mother know you well enough to serve as a compass, recognizing when you were not being true to *your* own nature?

## Mother as Cheerleader

When Mother is functioning as cheerleader, she is providing encouragement. This has some similarities to Mother as admiring mirror. The role is expanded here to include more active encouragement, praise, and support. The message is "You can do it! I know you can. We're behind you."

This support and encouragement is very important during the stage of exploration (eighteen months through three years of age) when the child is first moving into the world. We need someone who is not only behind us but also actively with us. In *Giving the Love That Heals: A Guide for Parents*, bestselling authors Harville Hendrix and Helen Hunt describe how a good mother does this. "She is consistently warm and available, taking time to allow the child to satisfy his curiosity and share it. She praises his successes and applauds his discoveries. She creates opportunities for him to discover more than he could on his own and makes a conscious effort for these explorations to be fun and filled with laughter."[7]

Cheerleader messages might also take the form of "I'm with you" or "I'm right here"—messages that are helpful when we're stepping into the world on wobbly feet.

We all need cheerleading at different times in life. It is especially helpful when we feel intimidated by a task. In cases where we may not have all the skills needed, it is most helpful when paired with Mother's role as mentor, which I discuss next.

A mother may have difficulty cheerleading for several reasons. She may be so undermothered and unsupported herself that she doesn't know about cheerleading, she may be more focused on her own needs for support, she may be unaware of her child's needs, or she may be threatened by her child's achievements and growing autonomy. She also may be too harried or depressed to have the energy to cheerlead.

Encouragement has to be tailored to the child and must be realistic. If there is encouragement but not enough support or if encouragement is paired with unrealistic expectations, it can be experienced as pushing. Encouragement for things already mastered, on the other hand, can leave you feeling patronized, as if Mother hasn't been paying attention and doesn't see your capacity.

When Mother does not celebrate our ordinary successes, we may feel invisible or that we have to accomplish extraordinary things (good or bad) to get her attention.

---

**Your mother as cheerleader**

➤ Do you think your mother was available and able to support your early discovery of the world?

➤ How was your mother at showing enthusiasm for your accomplishments? If she didn't do this well, what do you think may have gotten in her way?

➤ Do you believe that your mother had confidence in you? (You may have the sense that she believed in your capacities but just didn't don the cheerleading suit.)

➤ Can you think of a time when you needed more encouragement for something? What would you have liked to hear?

---

## Mother as Mentor

Imagine how terrifying it would be as a four- or five-year-old child to have someone put you on a bicycle and simply walk away. When Mother is there as mentor, she functions much like a set of training wheels. The role of training wheels is to help steady you while you're learning, to provide support so you don't fall on your face.

The function we're focusing on right now is that of support and guidance—calibrated help. We could also talk about Mother as teacher or guide. The task may at times involve modeling, such as showing a child how to ride a bicycle. Developmental psychologist and author Louise Kaplan uses the analogy of a stagehand in the theater. The stagehand helps with the behind-the-scenes support that allows someone else to perform successfully. Mother as Mentor provides enough support and guidance for us to develop our capacities.

Here Mother is teacher not simply of some isolated subject but of a much bigger curriculum. She orients the child to life and to successfully living in the world. She teaches her child how to get along with others, how to make good decisions, and how to manage time, meet responsibilities, and pursue goals. Mother is in this sense the first "life skills coach." Each of these capacities is huge, and any particular woman may be better at teaching some of them than others.

A mother will be more competent in some areas of life than others, and will also be helped or hindered by her teaching skills. Is she comfortable enough verbalizing that she can put skills into words, or does she teach only by example? Are her explanations clear and tailored to the child's needs and level of development? A mentor does not simply go through her life hoping that others will pick up what she knows, but is actively engaged in helping others learn. She is tuned in enough to notice what skills are needed and is patient enough to teach them.

We all know that you can help too much or too little. If you help too much, you take over and deprive the other of the chance to learn; if you help too little, the person feels overwhelmed and alone. Our efforts should be calibrated by the needs of those we're helping. In the case of parenting, it should also be age appropriate. It's one thing to help a child with homework or call up an elementary school teacher when some kind of advocacy is called for, and entirely another to call up the boss of your adult child when you think too much has been handed to him.

The Good Mother's guidance honors the child's limitations without drawing attention to them and without an attitude that the child should be one step ahead of where he is. Skillful guidance feels comforting rather than controlling or invasive.

I would add a further requirement for Mother as Mentor: understanding children's developmental needs and capacities. Many of the parents who have the most critical, punitive reactions to their children are those who expect too much and think the child is intentionally being obstinate—say, when she lacks the fine motor coordination needed to drink a glass of milk without spilling.

Being a good mentor thus requires several things:

- having developed skills yourself

- being able to break down a learning task into pieces and teach each step through clear verbal instruction and/or demonstration

- being attuned to the needs of the other

- having the time and patience required to mentor

This function has a great deal of overlap with Mother as Cheerleader: It takes encouragement and positive reinforcement for all of us to learn.

**Your mother as mentor**

➤ In what areas was your mother most engaged in mentoring you?
- getting along with peers
- learning to talk and articulate your experience
- understanding and managing feelings
- grooming and physical appearance
- learning to deal with gadgets, tools, technology
- showing respect for others ("manners")
- learning various social skills
- religious or spiritual education
- developing academic skills
- learning to take responsibility
- athletics or fitness
- good health habits
- arts and crafts
- homemaking skills
- critical thinking
- teaching you to be assertive and stand up for yourself
- handling disappointment and frustration

➤ Where did you need more mentoring than you got?

➤ Was her help calibrated to your needs? Did she help too much or too little?

➤ What attitudes were communicated through her help? (For example, that you were a bother, that she treasured you and wanted to help, that you could need help and still be deserving of respect, that you were a slow learner or quick learner, that she enjoyed teaching you . . .)

## Mother as Protector

How a mother provides protection for a child varies with different developmental stages. At first it involves providing a safe enclosure. The womb is the initial enclosure, and the symbiotic (undifferentiated) relationship is the second. Within this, the child does not feel separate, so the qualities of the mother's being and her feelings for the child are all part of the environment the baby exists within. The child needs to feel safe there.

With separateness comes danger. In the best of circumstances, Mother is there providing protection. A very young child often senses Mother as all-powerful. She shatters the darkness, shoos away noisy children and barking dogs. If the mother consistently protects the child from intrusive and overwhelming stimuli, the child feels safe. Mother here is morphing from safe enclosure to Mama Bear.

With more development, the child gains autonomy and the freedom to roam and explore, but the mother is never far away and at the first sign of danger is there fiercely protecting her offspring. The message associated with this function is "I'll keep you safe."

Still later, the child is sent out into the world with a set of rules and boundaries that are like an invisible fence, intended to keep the child out of harm's way. If children are not given these rules in a way that they can accept, or if they reject the rules as part of rejecting parental control, children are cast adrift, as their own judgment is often insufficient to protect them. To fully carry out this role of protector, a mother must teach her children about boundaries and self-protection.

Of course a mother can also be overprotective, not allowing her children as much room as they need to experience the world, or she can be protective in ways that communicate her mistrust in the child's capacities or perhaps her own mistrust of the world. How well Mother fulfills this role of protector cannot be reduced to only *whether* she provided protection but must also include *how* she provided it.

---

**Your mother as protector**

➤ What is your feeling reaction to imagining your mother as safe enclosure?

➤ What frustrations and dangers did she not adequately protect you from?

➤ Can you identify ways she did protect you?

➤ Did your mother teach you about protecting yourself? In what kinds of situations?

➤ What do you wish she taught you about self-protection that she did not?

➤ Did her way of protecting you feel more comforting to you or suffocating? Did it feel caring?

---

## Mother as Home Base

The message associated with this is "I'm here for you." When you really take that in, then even in adulthood you will reference Mother as the place you can always come back to for refueling, comfort, or support. When the world beats you down, when your marriage falls apart, when your feelings are hurt, you can always turn to Mother. This is similar to the period of development called *rapprochement,* where the child is first separating from Mother, venturing into the world, yet goes back and forth, back and forth, returning to Mother for psychological refueling.

Mother is our first home base, later replaced (or partially replaced if she maintains that role) by subsequent relationships and whatever we identify as *home*—be it community, country, place, or something else.

If Mother is not consistently available, is self-absorbed or absorbed elsewhere, is erratic and unstable or unable to be emotionally present for the child, then we don't experience her as home base. There is no Mother's lap. This may show up in adulthood as difficulty establishing a sense of home.

---

**Your mother as home base**

➤ Is Mother where you turn for comfort and refueling?

➤ If not, do you think she would be there if you did? Do you remember her being there for you?

➤ What attitudes come up in response to this item? Listen to the inner voices. Do they say, *Fat chance! Why would I turn to her?* or *I wish I could turn to her* or *Of course I can turn to her?*

---

When any one of these essential functions is missing, it leaves a hole in our development. Understanding what holes are there is a first step in eventually filling that hole. We will return to the issue of making up for specific deficits later in this book.

Working through this chapter may have left you feeling a bit glum. The vast majority of the undermothered have known few, if any, of these faces of the Good Mother. Please don't despair! None of these holes needs to be permanent. While it is true they will likely not be filled by the mother you grew up with, we can experience all of these functions somewhere in our adult lives.

# 3.

# Attachment: Our First Foundation

Our first interpersonal task in life is to bond with our primary caregiver, in most cases our mother. This is essential to our survival, since as babies we are totally dependent on someone to meet our basic needs. The term *attachment* is most often used when referring to this bond, and there has been a great deal of research into attachment behaviors and "styles." Attachment has significant impact on our brain development, mental health, and future relationships.

Although a child's relationship with his or her mother is not the only contributor to these things, it is the original and in most cases the primary influence. Fortunately, we can also form secure attachments with fathers, grandparents, nannies, day care workers, and others in a caretaking role, and we can form secure attachments in adulthood with mother figures, therapists, friends, and partners, thus reaping many of the benefits that bypassed us earlier.

### How do we become attached, and what is secure attachment?

Attachment begins in the first relationship of life, the relationship with Mother. This relationship begins early, even before birth, but is certainly shaped by the first hours, weeks, and

months of life. It can be heavily influenced by the circumstances of birth, including the parents' readiness and desire
for the baby, the mother's mental and emotional state around
birth, and birth procedures. (Studies show that mothers who
give birth by cesarean section take longer to attach to their babies.)[8] Even the levels of mothers' hormones have been found to
have an effect, with higher levels of oxytocin supporting more
attachment behaviors by mothers.[9] Many different ingredients
contribute to the quality of attachment between mother and
child.

Attachment is built through attunement and caring. In
the infant–mother relationship, it is spun largely out of the
infant's needs (expressed in what are called attachment behaviors) and the mother's responses to these needs. In fact the
mother's responses, their consistency and quality, are the key
ingredient.[10]

Research indicates that attachment is created not just
from meeting the immediate physical needs of the infant but
also from the *quality* of these interactions. The baby looks at
Mother, who is, in turn, looking at baby, and something passes
between them: a smile, a mirroring movement, a synchronized
dance way below the level of consciousness.

The most important caretaker behaviors associated with
secure attachment are these:

- Responding to the child's physical and emotional
  needs promptly, consistently, and in an attuned way.

- Responding to the child's attempts at closeness in a
  welcoming way. The mother must meet the child who
  is reaching for her, not turn away or provide only a cool
  reception. She must show that she wants closeness, too.

- Tuning in to the child's emotional states and
  demonstrating empathy.

- Looking at the child with love. One researcher reports that this is the most critical element in developing the part of the brain responsible for social behaviors.[11]

When we know that we can go to Mother and our needs will be met and our feelings will be understood and welcomed, we feel *secure* in that relationship. I have stated this as an older child might experience it, but the pattern is largely set in the first year of life, when our knowing is at a much more primitive level. Mother is either there or not there when we cry; she takes care of our needs, or she does not. In the developmental model of psychologist Erik Erikson, this relates to the basic sense of trust or mistrust that we develop in the first year of life. When the world (generally in the person of Mother) meets our needs consistently, we develop trust that we will have what we need and the world is perceived to be a safe place. This is what many today call *secure attachment.*

There is a significant amount of evidence that if a secure attachment is created in these early months and is not interrupted (by loss, by separations that are too much for the child, or by a loss of attunement), it will tend to be consistent throughout childhood.

## Why is attachment so important?

The attachment bond, which is the glue between the child and an attachment figure, is critical for many areas of development.

First, it very naturally affects self-esteem. "Secure individuals learn to perceive themselves as strong and competent, valuable, lovable, and special—thanks to being valued, loved, and viewed as special by caring attachment figures."[12] They score higher on every measure of self-esteem.[13]

Second, secure attachment gives us what is called a secure base, which means exactly what you might guess: the security needed to go into the world and explore it. When we don't feel this security, we're less ready to leave the nest or even to look inside ourselves, and thus are hampered in our development.

Author and therapist Susan Anderson describes how secure attachment allows for eventual independence:

> As a young child, you needed to connect in order to move forward. As an infant, you depended on your mother to give the nurturance you needed, and your attention focused almost exclusively on that relationship. When you were a toddler, she became a background object as you began to develop and function more independently.... If something interfered with that development—if Mommy had to go to the hospital for a long stay—your ability to function independently may have been delayed.[14]

Anderson goes on to explain that when your need for attachment is thwarted, it becomes primary; when satisfied, it blends into the background. Both children and adults with secure attachment aren't hung up on getting other people to see or support them and can focus on meeting other needs.

In addition to providing a secure base from which we can explore the world and attend to other things, attachment correlates with a number of long-term effects. Studies show that securely attached children have enhanced emotional flexibility, social functioning, and cognitive abilities.[15] They are better at initiating.[16] As middle school children, they handle frustration and challenge better, and when they start falling behind, they try harder rather than collapse as insecure children do.[17] Secure children become well-adjusted adults with the ability to form secure attachments and regulate their emotions, and they hold a positive outlook on the world.[18]

In contrast, a number of studies suggest that the various forms of insecurity of attachment can be associated with emotional rigidity, difficulty in social relationships, impairments in attention, difficulty in understanding the minds of others, and risk in the face of stressful situations.[19]

The latter is because the stress response is less healthy in those with insecure attachment. Stress response plays a role in our susceptibility to many mental and physical illnesses. The stress response is mediated by the hormone cortisol, and insecurely attached children are disadvantaged by having too much of it circulating. High levels of cortisol have been associated with depression, anxiety, suicidal tendencies, eating disorders, and alcoholism. Too much cortisol can damage parts of the brain responsible for retrieving information and thinking clearly.[20] High cortisol is also believed to contribute to insomnia.

Researchers have been studying how the interactions that are the basis of secure attachment affect brain development and functioning.[21] The area of the brain most involved in complex social behaviors (so much so that it is sometimes referred to as the social brain) is particularly sensitive to these early interactions. It will sound like an oversimplification, but these caring, attuned interactions actually grow this part of our brains, which is responsible for important social abilities and social intelligence.[22]

So considering everything from the growth of neurons to one's sense of self-esteem, the security of our attachment is very important. Some consider this the most critical of all childhood needs.

**How can I know if I was securely attached to my mother?**
You won't know precisely what your relationship with your mother was in your earliest years, but here are some important clues:

- moments from your early relationship that were captured in memories

- your current feelings about your early relationship with your mother

- your patterns in relationships throughout your life and specifically your ability to form strong bonds with others

Since this last item is complex, it will take some time to get a clear picture of it. First, let's explore your early relationship with your mother:

➤ Do you have memories of close moments, her holding you lovingly, smiling and expressing affection? If so, do they seem like moments that were the exception or the rule?

➤ Do you have memories of going to your mother in times of need? What kinds of need? Is this representative of typical childhood needs? How did your mother respond?

➤ As far as you can remember or checking in with your feeling response, were your attempts at closeness welcomed?

➤ What descriptions have you heard about yourself as a baby and small child?

You may not be able to remember much about your early relationships, yet your feelings and impulses are often clues, leftovers from interactions you can't consciously recall. They have something to teach you. Listen, if you can.

## What if I wasn't securely attached? How would that look?

If you weren't securely attached, you've got a fair amount of company. Research indicates that about one third of children experience insecure attachment, which tends to be transmitted from one generation to the next.[23] This number climbs to half in children whose mothers are depressed.[24]

A number of "styles" of insecure attachment have been described. Since various writers in the field use different terms to describe these styles, it sometimes gets confusing. For each style, I have chosen the term that seems most memorable and descriptive and included the equivalent terms that the better-known researchers have used.

### Self-sufficient style

The largest of the insecure categories is a style that has been called by several names—*compulsively self-sufficient* (Bowlby), *avoidant* (Ainsworth), and *dismissive* (Main, referring to this style in adults).

When the mother is consistently rejecting or nonresponsive and emotionally unavailable, the child gives up, learns it is futile or dangerous in relationships to need, and consequently turns off his or her needs and attachment feelings. This, in essence, is what this style is all about.

More specifically, mothers of avoidant children have been found to:

- reject the infant's needs for attachment and the behaviors the infant shows to try to get attachment

- be uncomfortable or hostile toward signs of dependency

- dislike affectionate, face-to-face contact

- be more aversive to cuddly contact and physical contact

- show less emotion[25]

When mothers don't show enjoyment when holding their babies, babies eventually seem to turn off their more natural desire to be cuddled. When held, they tend to go limp like a sack of potatoes.

These children have "turned off wanting." Of course you can't fully turn off wanting; you just disconnect from your awareness of it. Your wanting gets relegated to the unconscious, where it remains in very primitive form and has a sense of great urgency attached to it.

Children in this situation perceive that their parents don't want to deal with their needs and feelings and learn to conceal their emotions, especially from caretakers they are avoidantly attached to. The same child who goes limp like a sack of potatoes as an infant is the school-aged child with one-word responses when Mother asks about his day and who keeps Mother at arm's length. This child will not go to Mother for help. Even if she wanted to connect more with him later, the child is now on guard, hidden behind a wall.

Cutting off feelings has costs. Without the caregiver noticing and responding to feelings, children—and later adults—will have a harder time noticing their own feelings and putting them into words. They also won't be good at having a nuanced understanding of other people's feelings.[26] As you can imagine, the lack of feeling awareness and feeling talk will hamper them in later intimate relationships, where they will appear more cloaked and cut off. Just as with wanting, their feelings won't go away but rather lurk beneath consciousness.

People who predominantly have this attachment style have turned off their attachment needs and, as one researcher suggests, become deaf to attachment-related signals.[27] Better to be as self-sufficient as possible. A person with this style is more armored in relationships and tends to not allow much closeness. Letting others close enough to develop real feelings of attachment even much later in life feels scary; it is too close to the unbearable pain of feeling rejected as an infant when one was so utterly dependent.

## Preoccupied style

A different expression of insecure attachment consists of what we more traditionally think of as insecure behaviors, such as clinging, needing reassurance, and always wanting more closeness. The chief fear in this pattern is of the attachment figure leaving, what we might call a fear of abandonment. Of course the self-sufficient type fears abandonment, too, but protects herself by not letting the relationship feel as important as it is to her.

This second style has been called *anxious attachment* (Bowlby), *compulsive care seeking, ambivalent* (Ainsworth), *dependent,* and *preoccupied.* All of these names reflect some important quality in the pattern. The dependence and care seeking are obvious; the ambivalence, slightly more complex. Children with this style show both a heightened need for closeness *and* an angry, rejecting quality. In the Strange Situation, a much-used research design, these children as one-year-olds are extremely distressed at being left by Mother but have a difficult time accepting her ministrations when she tries to patch things up. They go back and forth between being very demanding and clingy and being hostile. I've chosen the term *preoccupied* because through both sets of behaviors, these children (and later adults) are so anxiously tied up with how available others are that it dominates their lives.

This style of attachment has been correlated with mothers who are less consistently rejecting than the self-sufficient children had, but not consistently responsive enough to create secure attachment. Sometimes they're there; sometimes they're not. Sometimes they are experienced as loving; other times, as inexplicably rejecting. The preoccupied child (and later adult) doesn't know what to expect.

Insecure attachment styles are actually strategies for managing the uncomfortable emotions aroused by Mother's inconsistency, according to author Diana Fosha. "Their coping style—

watching Mother like a hawk and clinging to her to reassure themselves she won't disappear again—is their way of managing their fear and pain associated with the inconsistency."[28]

Unfortunately the strategies used to secure the desired attachment often drive people away. By the time we reach adulthood, these include:

- heightened needs for closeness

- hypervigilance about attachment signals

- always questioning and testing the other's commitment

- emphasizing need and helplessness in order to get others to stay

- punishing others for not providing what is desired

- anger when attachment needs are not met

Being alone, especially during times of distress, is upsetting for those with anxious attachment, and they don't do well when their attachment figures go away. In later relationships, they are likely to feel insecure when their romantic partner goes away, and more likely to be jealous. Those with this attachment style are always looking for love.[29]

Children with this style appear too caught up in attachment concerns to explore their world, and there is some evidence that adults with this style are so preoccupied with relationships that they turn into underachievers.[30]

Sometimes people show elements of both of these patterns: for example, alternating between cutting off feelings and plunging into them headlong, or acting detached and self-sufficient and then collapsing into a dependent pattern. What is common to all forms of insecure attachment is a lack of confidence that others will be emotionally available and can be counted on to provide support.

## Caretaker style

Another pattern identified in attachment theory is called *compulsive caregiving*. In this pattern you deny your own needs and focus on the other person's.[31] You help other people (whether they want it or not) as a way to be close to them. It is associated with mothers who were not able to provide for their children but welcomed their children's caretaking of them.[32]

Most modern attachment theorists don't include this style, and there is some evidence pairing a caretaker style in adulthood with a preoccupied style as a child,[33] which makes intuitive sense, since caretaking is one way to maintain connection.

## Disorganized style

Some children fit a pattern that is called *disorganized* or *disoriented* attachment. Here, there isn't a consistent pattern. These children show behaviors characteristic of one or more other attachment styles alternating with moments of confusion and fear. This is the pattern found in the majority of children who are abused.

Of course abusive parents aren't only abusive; sometimes they provide needed care. So they are both a source of fear and a source of reassurance, and this is understandably confusing.[34]

The behavior of the child is likewise inconsistent. Such a child may appear confused or apprehensive in the presence of that parent and even dazed at times. How can you know whether it's safe to go to Mommy if sometimes she comforts you and other times she seems to spiral out of control and hits you? And why is she sometimes so spaced out? (Neglectful and abusive parents are often untreated trauma victims.)

Disorganized attachment is also often found in children whose parents abuse alcohol or drugs, or are chronically depressed.[35]

These children are often found to take on caretaking roles with their parents, in essence abandoning the child role altogether. It's a pretty smart response, if you think about it. Children in these situations often see that adults can't really be trusted or aren't very competent, so taking a provider role is probably safer.

Some of the effects associated with disorganized attachment include:

- marked impairments in emotional, social, and cognitive functioning[36]

- not being able to soothe yourself[37]

- feeling that you are to blame for what was done to you and that you are of no value[38]

- feeling alienated from the world around you

- being vigilant and distrustful, avoiding intimacy[39]

- use of dissociation, distraction, and/or aggression or withdrawal as coping mechanisms[40]

- smaller brain size and damage to fibers connecting the two sides of the brain[41]

While disorganized attachment is the most insecure of the attachment styles that have been identified, it is not the same as an *attachment disorder,* a term that refers to a condition of nonattachment and most often refers to *reactive attachment disorder* (RAD). With RAD, a child does not develop an attachment relationship with primary caregivers or easily develop relationship with anyone. It is associated with severe early neglect, abuse, abrupt separation from caregivers before three years of age, and frequent change of caregivers.

## What is attachment-related trauma?

There are a number of things related to parents or other attachment figures that are traumatic for a child. For a young child, being left alone is traumatic.[42] A separation that is more than the child can handle is traumatic. Significant disruptions in the attachment relationship or loss of an attachment figure is traumatic. Physical or sexual abuse by an attachment figure is traumatic.

Being abandoned as a child in times of urgent need is also traumatic and leads to attachment injuries. An example is telling a parent that another parent is abusing you, and having the parent you tell not believe you or either ignore or minimize what you've said and not protect you. Remember, your relationships with attachment figures are where you're supposed to learn that the world is safe. Secure attachment grows from your needs being met. Not being protected or being overlooked in a state of emergency will be felt as abandonment and perhaps a violation.

Trauma at any age is devastating (see my book *Healing from Trauma*), but when you combine it with an attachment figure its mark is nearly indelible.

## Maybe I wasn't securely attached to my mother, but is it really fair to hold her responsible?

Although children come into the world with significant differences, there is considerable support for the notion that the caretaker's behavior is critical in forming secure attachment. Particularly telling is the fact that an infant may be securely attached to one parent and insecurely attached to another. When this is the case, the infant clearly has the capacity to attach, given proper responsiveness.

There is evidence that coaching mothers and helping them become more responsive to their child can alter the attachment pattern. In a short time, improvements in a mother's attuned responsiveness lead to increasingly secure attachment in their children.[43]

Holding Mother responsible for our insecure attachment is not saying that she is somehow bad or even uncaring. There are many things that may be going on. For one, she may love her baby but feel frightened or repulsed by being needed. Unfortunately this often leads to a vicious cycle, because the more she withdraws or withholds her care, the more the baby signals his need, and it is this signaling of need and the urgency behind it that may frighten the mother. Other contributors include being unskilled at reading a baby's signals; being preoccupied, overwhelmed, or depressed; being insecure and overly sensitive to rejection; and having been undermothered herself. If her mother was not able to graciously give to her or attune to her needs, if her mother was too busy or too cold, then this is the pattern branded into her, which she unwittingly repeats. Often people find it elicits deep hurt and is hard to tolerate when others receive what was so painfully missing for them, and mothers are subject to this, too.

We'll talk later about coming to a more objective understanding of what was going on with your mother, but for now it's better to give the responsibility for your early relationship and attachment style to her than to somehow wonder what you did wrong. Even when you were part of the dance, as in the complicated situation where both mother and child mirror each other's turning away, it is the mother, as the adult, who has the greater responsibility to become aware and change the pattern.

### Can I still develop secure attachments if I've only partially done so in the past? How would this help me?

Even if you have never had a secure attachment, it's never too late to develop one. There are many benefits to secure attachment. They include:

- giving you an anchor in the world, a place where you are connected

- supporting a more positive picture of people and more optimistic sense about your life

- helping to build a sense of security that you keep with you

- offering you a place to rest, where you are not alone but rather held by another

- providing a platform of good feelings that strengthens self-esteem and confidence

- making it more likely that you can reach out to others in the future with your needs

- strengthening favorable neural pathways and stimulating brain development

- improving your capacity to self-regulate (p. 27)

- giving you an important resource that helps you know you can handle the rough spots on the bumpy road of life

Developing secure attachments with trustworthy others is important in healing the deficits left by undermothering.

**Identifying attachment figures**
Often as adults our attachment figures are intimate partners, but they may also include therapists or other helpers, mother substitutes, and best friends. Some children have imaginary friends who perhaps fill some of these needs, and many people—adults as well as children—rely on pets for a sense of comfort and connection.

If you are unsure who might be serving as an attachment figure for you or potentially could, here are some questions to ask yourself:

> Who do I feel comfortable going to when I am most upset? Who can I go to in times of need?

> Who do I trust really cares about how I'm doing? Who cares about me for *me* (and not what I give them)?

> If I were in a state of almost complete dependency (say, after a major accident or illness), who would I want to be with?

> Who can I trust to be consistently there for me?

You might also reflect on your childhood and who you could depend on then.

## What is my attachment style?

If you haven't already identified yourself with a particular attachment style, you might find it interesting to read the following descriptions and see which is more like you. Note that these are oriented toward adults and close relationships rather than the infant–mother relationship.[44] I've also limited them to three items each. Research scales have been developed that are quite long, but this small sample can give you a taste.

### Style A:

- I often worry that romantic partners don't really love me or won't want to stay with me.

- Sometimes my desire for closeness scares other people away.

- I more often want greater closeness than my partner wants.

### Style B:

- I don't like to have to depend on others. It feels like a setup for being hurt.

- I would rather not show my vulnerability to others. In fact, I would rather not *feel* vulnerable!

- I am nervous when someone gets too close to me.

### Style C:

- I am comfortable depending on others and having them depend on me.

- I find it relatively easy to get close to people.

- I trust that others will be there (most of the time) when I need them.

### Style D:

- I get close to others by meeting their needs.

- I think that if I meet enough of their needs, they won't leave me.

- There doesn't seem to be room for both of our needs.

It is quite obvious, but for the record, A is the preoccupied style, B is self-sufficient, C represents secure attachment, and D is compulsive caregiving. Since disorganized attachment is the absence of a clear style, it is much harder to self-identify using an instrument such as this.

There are many ways to dig deeper into your attachment style, and I'll mention a few other things that you may notice in your life now.

One interesting clue is how you respond to perceived abandonment. Some of the early research in attachment styles was done by having mothers leave their toddlers for a brief time and then reenter the room (the Strange Situation). The children with the more defended, detached style (self-sufficient) had the hardest time reconnecting when Mother came back. Often they ignored her. These children, in essence, communicated, "Oh, you. You're not important to me." Instead, they focused on what they were doing.

Notice what your style has been in situations in which someone you are attached to has left. Does it feel too vulnerable to show loved ones that you miss them, or do you find it hard when they go away (as the self-sufficient do)? Do you find it hard to warm up again when they return? Are you so focused on the loss that it's hard to let it go when the person returns (as is typical of preoccupied, ambivalent attachment)? Do you want to punish them for having been gone (as the preoccupied/ambivalent are more prone to do)? In the research described above, it was young children's response to reconnecting with their mothers more than how they responded to separations that was most indicative of their attachment style.

I believe our basic security or insecurity also gets reflected by our response to disappointment and hurt in important relationships. What happens for you when someone has disappointed you? Maybe you were expecting to receive an acknowledgment of an important event in your life and it was totally forgotten. Do you feel crushed, even if the oversight was minor? Do you pull your heart back a little? Do you want to punish the other in some small way? Do you try to make it unimportant to you and hide your disappointment, or can you show it? Secure attachments build more resilience and allow us to be more expressive. I would expect those with a more self-sufficient style to hide feelings of hurt and disappointment (as well as desire for closeness) and those with the preoccupied style to perhaps accentuate such feelings, using guilt if needed, in an effort to create a more secure relationship. (I am focusing on these two subtypes of insecurity, as they are the most researched and talked about.)

### Can I have more than one style?
You can certainly have characteristics of more than one of these styles. Rather than focus too exclusively on these categories, it may be more helpful to look at various spectrums that can be associated with them, such as your comfort with dependency and showing vulnerability, your capacity for closeness, your ability to handle feelings, and your sense of security and being wanted—all matters we'll continue to address in later chapters.

It may also be helpful to think about these as qualities of particular relationships. Just as a child may show different attachment styles with each parent, we show an assortment of attachment-related qualities in our various adult relationships. The value of looking at styles is to illuminate these elements and discover patterns. It's also valuable to consider that these patterns were first established in our most significant early relationships.

### Does my relationship with my mother really affect later relationships?

Whether you had no relationship with your mother, had a secure and happy one, or fall somewhere in between, it is impossible to escape the influence of this central relationship.

What happened to you as an infant and young child powerfully shapes how you see yourself and other people, what expectations you have for relationships, how you feel about yourself, and what defensive (and healthy!) habits you've learned.

For example, if you enjoyed secure attachment, you learned that showing your needs for closeness or comfort or expressing your needs in general was okay; in fact, it was the basis of forming relationships. If, however, your mother (or mothering figure) pretty consistently rejected these bids for affection, support, and protection, you learned not only to stop showing these needs but also to cut off your own awareness of them (self-sufficient style). If Mother was inconsistent, sometimes responding positively and sometimes not, you may have learned that the only way to make sure your attachment needs are met is to keep focused on them, keep close tabs on the people you are in relationships with, and continue highlighting your feelings and needs (preoccupied style).

Take a moment now to reflect on your own situation.

> ➤ From what you've learned so far, what can you see about your pattern of showing or not showing attachment needs? How does this relate to your experiences as an adolescent and adult?

> ➤ How does this relate to the attachment patterns you imagine you had as a child with your mother?

## How difficult is it to change attachment patterns?

It is easiest to change insecure attachment patterns as a child. I've mentioned that coaching mothers to better attune to their infants can have very rapid positive results. The longer a pattern is in place within a particular relationship, the harder it is to reverse.

Insecurely attached children are thought to be relatively amenable to change throughout their early years, although this is primarily tied to their ability to develop a secure attachment that helps offset (and provides an alternative to) their insecure attachment with their mother.[45] Research has shown that a secure attachment to the father (or to another secondary caregiver) is the most important factor in children compensating for or overcoming an insecure attachment to the mother.[46]

It's considered a bit tougher as an adult to change our fundamental pattern of attachment, but by then we have a new set of options. We're more able to do the therapeutic work involved in grieving old wounds, uncovering core beliefs, and establishing new ways of being. Having relationships that create new, healthier patterns can change our expectations and attitudes and give us a new foundation from which to work. We'll talk more about all of this in later chapters.

Remember, we are wired to form attachment relationships. It is how nature intended it.

# 4.

# More Building Blocks

Attachment is only one of the many building blocks that make us who we are. In this chapter we'll do a quick review of the secure relationship and then proceed to other elements that help support a child's developing sense of self.

## Feeling safe and secure

Safety and security are experienced somewhat differently for a child than for many adults—although, as some have noted, in times of emergency we all want contact (including touch) with the people most important to us. When the bombs are flying, we cling to those we hold most dear.

For the young child, safety is being enveloped in an attuned, caring environment. It's not about locks on the doors but the sense that "Mommy will watch out for me, Mommy will remember me. I'm precious to her, and she's not going to forget about me." If Mommy is preoccupied, distracted, or annoyed and doesn't provide this, the child feels less safe. When you are dependent, security is feeling that the person you rely on is dependable.

To appreciate the vulnerability of dependency, imagine that you are flying in a plane that has only one pilot—and you realize that the pilot is drunk. Or you're just going under for surgery, and it dawns on you that the surgeon doesn't know what she is doing. For the young child with an emotionally absent mother, it's like discovering the captain of the ship is just a mannequin and not really human.

The child's sense of safety is built from many things—feeling the mother's competence, sensing her attunement to the child, and feeling held. Writing from the perspective of a very young inner child, one woman recorded this in her journal:

> I want to be held in a pink blanket with support all around me. I want to feel securely held, securely contained. Secure. That seems like a new feeling. Wrapped in a warm, safe place with lots of protection around me. . . . If I was securely contained, I wouldn't need to hold myself together.

This last phrase is interesting given the comment by pediatrician and psychoanalyst D. W. Winnicott, who said that the mother "holds the child's bits together." She is his glue, his container. When the mother is really there, lovingly holding the child, it gives the child something to hold on to. Ultimately, that is the mother's heart.

It's worth repeating that this sense of security provided by the relationship, this secure base, is what makes it safe for the child to explore the world. When we have a safe place to come back to, we can leave, just as when we are securely held, we don't need to cling. Research shows that secure babies explore when they feel safe and seek connection when they do not. This is our innate programming.

Not feeling safe, on the other hand, is the setup for anxiety to take hold. Anxiety, which is seen by many in the mental health fields as the basis of unhealthy defenses and the root of psychopathology, starts here. It comes from feeling alone and unsupported in situations we can't handle by ourselves and from being in relationships with unavailable or unresponsive caregivers.[47]

## A happy home

For the child, the secure relationship with Mother is a first-level container for her growth, and a happy home is a larger, second container. It would be like a houseplant potted in good soil and then kept in a room with the right light and temperature.

A happy home is a place that feels good to be in. People feel friendly toward one another and at peace within themselves. Members recognize that the family is a cooperative unit in which everyone's needs and satisfaction are important, and, as a child, you feel that your needs are considered right at the top of the list. Knowing this gives you a place. It gives you support for having needs and for being yourself.

In a happy home, there aren't continuing crises you need to solve (or wonder how to endure when you're too young to solve anything). People aren't stuck in power struggles. There aren't silent or not-so-silent wars between family members. In a happy home you're not all holding your breath. You can relax and be yourself.

A happy home may have a second parent (not necessarily of the opposite sex), but it doesn't have to. It helps Mommy be happy if she has the support of other important adults. It certainly doesn't help her when there is ongoing friction in those relationships. In a happy home there may or may not be other children, may or not be pets. In a home steeped in the feelings of strain and deprivation, more beings to take care of saps a mother, but in a happy home Mother seems to have enough to provide for everyone without resentment. She seems to enjoy giving! (This may be a shock for those whose experience has been quite different.)

Feeling that Mommy is happy is a great boon to a child. Imagine for a moment a snapshot of Mother smiling and laughing. She's happy to be here. She's happy with you and anyone else in the picture, and she doesn't need things to be any different than they are in that moment. She is relaxed! When Mommy is relaxed and smiling, we sense that her world is right. And when her world is right, then our world is right.

But when Mommy is distracted or worried or depressed, we don't have the same kind of support, and it's harder for us to relax and be fully present. It doesn't feel quite right to be expansive and expressive when Mommy is withdrawn or frazzled. There isn't really a place to be happy, unless we're putting on a happy face trying to cheer Mother up. Mother's happiness relieves us of these burdens, and we can simply express ourselves as we are.

### When things go wrong, they can be fixed!

A happy, healthy home is not without problems, but these problems can be fixed rather than swept under the rug where they build into huge mounds. Conflicts are resolved, and there are competent adults who can problem-solve a variety of needs.

This is critically important in the arena of relationships. A child needs to know that there can be angry feelings and times of falling-out, but these ruptures can be repaired. In chapter 1, I described how the good-enough mother is frequently off the mark and that repairing ruptures in relationships again and again is part of securing the bond and creating a sense of resilience. This is true whether we're talking about the mother–child bond, a therapist–client relationship, a relationship with a partner, or any significant relationship. We need to know that the other can manage the upsetting feelings that come with such ruptures and won't go away, and that together we'll fix it.

We don't know this without experience. I remember how shocked I was in a therapy session when my frustration and anger finally burst out against my therapist—and my next thought was that I could now kiss our relationship good-bye. I apparently held a belief that if I expressed my anger, I would destroy our bond forever. The relationship was not ruined; in fact, it was strengthened. But I had no reference, no previous experience to tell me this could be so. I had never dared express my anger at my family and had a marked lack of experience in this process of rupture and repair.

Knowing that ruptures can be repaired is another aspect of secure attachment and contributes to a child's sense of resilience.

## A sense of belonging

Many factors go into creating a sense of belonging for a child. There are obvious external things, like sharing the same name, having the same home, and perceiving a likeness with family members—sharing the same eyes or nose or mouth.

Secure attachment creates a deep sense of belonging, because it anchors you, giving you a place in the web of life. That place is bigger than any one relationship, but Mother as our first relationship sets the stage. Later, we may find belonging by knowing that we are part of a team, a tribe, a neighborhood, a club, a community, a nation, or a social movement—or by having our own children and mate. When we have a sense of belonging at several of these levels, we feel embedded, part of something.

Feeling valued and known are also part of this belonging. If a family claims you as their own but you don't really feel that they know you or see you for who you are, you'll feel like an outsider within your own family.

## The budding self

A baby's emerging self is highly impressionable, and a good mother knows that. She treats it with utmost care and respect, just as she treats the growing bond between them. Their interactions are like passing a shuttle of yarn back and forth, weaving a connection between their hearts.

These interactions are critical in shaping the sense of self. The baby's sense of self does not yet take the form of a separate individual but is steeped in the feelings of the relationship with Other—in this case, with Mother.

Mother is the facilitator of the child's developing self, and her support and encouragement of the child's emerging qualities are essential. For the child's "true self" to have a chance to take hold, it needs to be seen. The only way the child knows that she is seen is by other people mirroring back her feelings and experiences, acknowledging and celebrating them. If the child's unique qualities are not mirrored or supported, they are not available for her as a foundation. Instead of becoming grounded in her own nature, she adapts to what she thinks she is supposed to be, taking on a false self. For some people, this false self (which we all have to some degree) so obscures everything else that it's all they know.

## A place to grow

If we are to have any chance at becoming our true self, we need an environment in which we can grow into ourselves, one that provides the ingredients we need in order to develop fully. Just as insufficient minerals in the soil will dwarf a plant's growth and change its character, insufficient nutrients in the early environment stunt our development.

These nutrients include unconditional acceptance ("I accept you just as you are"), respect, and value, in addition to the mirroring and attuned responsiveness already discussed. You need to be valued for who you are and also valued simply because of the fact *that* you are. If you don't get this, you feel out of place and like you don't belong. This makes it hard to embrace life.

What is respected and valued in a particular family is what gets reinforced. Here is an exercise to explore this.

➤ Look at the following list and note which of these your
   family valued.
- intelligence
- mastery and achievement
- sweetness
- innocence
- delicacy
- sensitivity
- hardiness
- humor and silliness
- being tough
- being affectionate
- needing others
- being confident and, on occasion, "full of yourself"
- being in your body in a sensual way, enjoying your
   contact with the world
- being attractive
- helping behaviors
- expression of feelings
- imagination and creativity

➤ Note which of these same qualities were disregarded,
   almost as if they didn't exist. Which were mocked
   or belittled? What can you see about this? What
   happened to those qualities that were not valued when
   you were growing up?

We can give ourselves a new experience, creating new
options, just by working deeply with imagination. To do this,
select a quality that was not supported, and then imagine
someone important to you recognizing this quality in you and
really celebrating it. Imagine this person saying that it is one
of the things he or she likes most about you. Notice what you
feel in response. Take that feeling all the way in, experiencing
it in your body.

Often we need to work through our own rejection of the qualities that were not valued and fight for the right to have these qualities or behave in these ways.

## Support for being a child

Think about the characteristics that are simply part of being a very young child. These include the following:

- being dependent

- having needs

- having limited tolerance for frustration, needing things to be just right for us

- being innocent and naïve

- being undeveloped and without mastery

- expressing emotions quite immediately and authentically

- seeking closeness and affection

- being delicate and sweet

Aren't these characteristics universally found in children of all cultures and conditions if they are not censured?

Now the more telling question: Aren't these the very qualities that are often ignored or rejected in our families? To the extent this is so, we are valued not for being a child, but for growing out of it.

Of course we need our parents to cheer us on and value our growing independence and mastery, but too often for the undermothered there has been more support for this side of development than for these innate characteristics of being a child. There is often more interest in our outgrowing early childhood needs than there is in meeting these needs.

There may be numerous reasons that parents reject these "softer" qualities. In their own development, they often had to skip over this same stage as quickly as possible. A woman whose sweetness got no support as a little girl, for example, will find it difficult to embrace her child's sweetness. It rubs up against her own wound. This is true for dependency, sensitivity, and the other softer qualities. Maybe a mother's innocence was torn away from her by early hardship or abuse and she blamed herself for being open and undefended. She will see this condition as dangerous and feel uncomfortable when her child seems vulnerable.

There may be times when undue stress and hardship interfere with a mother's ability to nurture these softer qualities, but often the culprit lies in her own childhood experience. Also, if she was expected to grow up fast and quickly leave childhood needs and limitations behind, she often will have an unrealistic expectation of what her child is capable of. It is these mothers who often become angry and abusive.

> ➤ Looking again at the innate characteristics of a young child, which of these do you think your parents supported?

> ➤ What, if anything, do you think made it difficult for your mother to embrace these softer qualities?

To develop naturally, we need to grow at our own pace. In fact, forced growth, pressured growth, is often distorted growth. To eventually grow beyond childhood, we first need support for being a child.

## Touch

Nurturing, caring touch is an important building block in developing not only a sense of self but also a self that has value. It is such an essential need that babies deprived of touch often die.

You perhaps have heard of failure to thrive (FTT) syndrome, which was discovered years ago in orphanages. The babies whose bassinets were at the end of the line withered and died at a much higher rate than those near the front of the line, even though all were being fed. This syndrome was drastically reduced when researchers realized that the difference was that those at the far end were not being picked up and receiving the attention the others were, and they then had people come in and remedy this.

Nurturing touch has all sorts of physiological benefits, including promoting the growth of the nervous system, stimulating the immune system, and decreasing stress hormones, but let's focus on the emotional and psychological value. It is through nurturing touch that we feel loved, soothed, protected.

Appropriate touch also helps us locate ourselves in our bodies. The untouched child may be alienated from his or her own body and experience feelings of unreality.[48] The sense of reality comes from being grounded in the body, and touch is part of what accomplishes this. A lack of touch or abusive touch may also encourage dissociation, a psychic separation from the body.

Paradoxically, a lack of touch can also lead to a sense of imprisonment within the body. In *Touching: The Human Significance of the Skin,* Ashley Montagu writes, "It is in large part the stimulation of his skin by touch which enables the child to emerge from his own skin." He explains how a child who has not been sufficiently touched becomes locked inside his own skin and then experiences normal touch as threatening.[49] This is called *tactile defensiveness.* Such defensiveness can manifest as insensitivity or hypersensitivity to being touched or in being touch-avoidant.

Children who do not receive enough positive touch will often (unconsciously) feel untouchable, as if there must be something terribly wrong with them. Negative touch often occurs as rough disciplinary touch or hostility, neither of which communicates any sense of valuing the child. Young children don't have the cognitive development to understand that parental misbehavior and failings have nothing to do with them. In general, the earlier the touch deprivation, the more devastating it is.

There are many reasons that mothers may be uncomfortable touching their children. If they haven't received enough nurturing touch themselves, they may have become tactilely defensive and may not be very present in their body. Nurturing touch may feel unfamiliar to them, not part of their repertoire. Because of abuse or other factors they may be uncomfortable with their own body and with other bodies, including those of their children. A mother who feels shame about her body will often pass that down to her offspring.

Here are some questions to help you explore this:

➤ What touch was available to you as a child? (You may want to think of yourself at different ages.)

➤ If your mother didn't seem comfortable with touch, why do you think that is?

➤ If you feel you have not had sufficient touch, how has this affected you? Do you crave contact and sometimes do not-so-safe things to get it? Are you comfortable receiving touch of various kinds?

➤ If you weren't touched much, what did you make of this experience? Do you resonate with the feeling of being untouchable?

## Love is the medium, love is the message

We could say that touch is the medium and love is the message, but love is also a medium in the sense that it is the best soil for a child's growth. Every heart is nurtured by love and opens as it accepts love. Being loved makes one more loving. It also helps create resilience.

Love is communicated not just through touch, but also by tone of voice, facial expression, responsiveness, words, and quality of care. A child can feel how much (or how little) love is there.

When present, love informs other kinds of mothering behaviors like protection, encouragement, support, and guidance. For example, when love is absent, there may be a carelessness and lack of appropriate protection or there may be protective limits that are experienced as restrictive and unfair. When limits are set without love, a child may perceive such limits as a power trip. When encouragement is given but the child doesn't feel love, it may feel like pushing rather than supporting; the child may even feel that the parents want his or her success for their own glorification. Thus, without love, nothing works well, and with love even the clumsiest parenting can be forgiven.

Now that we've talked about the building blocks and the many essential functions that a good mother provides, let's turn to the question of what happens when these are missing.

# 5.

# Mommy, Where Were You?

Young children do not have the perspective to understand all the external factors that influence people's behavior. They mistakenly believe that when others hurt or abandon them, it must be because of something they did. They conclude that they must be bad or unlovable. The feeling at fault isn't always conscious, but it's usually there on some level. We see it at the end of the poem that opened this book, "Mommy, Where Were You?" when the child asks, "Was it because of me?"

## The hole where Mother was supposed to be

To feel that you aren't important to your mother leaves a hole. Most often it is felt as a hole in the heart. It's the hole where Mother was supposed to be.

On close examination, there are three layers to this. The first layer is the outer one related to the external lack. Here the absence of mother may be evident in unsupervised, undernurtured, undersocialized children. It shows up in children whose development is a bit slower than it needs to be because they haven't gotten the individual attention and support for their growth of language, motor skills, and earliest academic skills.

The second layer is the hole in the sense of self that results from being undermothered. If we want to be precise, we can view this as a family of holes. There is the hole left by feeling unloved, the hole left when you're not mirrored and consequently don't feel fully real, the hole in your confidence that results from a lack of encouragement and praise, the sense of not belonging anywhere, and the hole of feeling homeless, among others.

One undermothered adult described to me the severe love hunger she was left with. "When there's a hole in your heart, you can't get enough," she told me. Since she was premature at birth, she had been put in an incubator and missed out on the contact she would have normally had. This left her with a craving both for loving touch and for any kind of positive attention. Throughout her youth and young adulthood, she felt an intense need for affection and developed crushes on anyone who gave her any kind of positive recognition.

Sometimes this hole results in an extreme loneliness. One woman remembers at age four feeling a wave of loneliness and thinking, *It's the I-don't-have-a-mother feeling.* The rational part of her then countered that she did have a mother, so it was confusing.

The third layer comes into view when we look at how we mother ourselves and find the same deficits that were present in our actual mothers. We see that we don't know how to support or encourage ourselves, don't know how to be patient and tender, don't know how to take into account our needs and limitations. Here, there is a hole in our inner mother.

This book is concerned with all three layers of this hole. By explaining what a good mother provides and asking how this compares with your experience, you can see which capacities were lost or underdeveloped. The healing chapters (7–12) are about filling these holes. Developing the inner mother gets the most attention in chapters 9 and 10.

Our memories of Mother being there or not being there begin very early. One woman's first memory is of lying on a blanket, reaching up with her arms until eventually she drops them because no one comes. This is an exercise sometimes done in workshops—to lie like an infant and reach and call for help. Some carry such wounds that they are unable to do this. A very telling finding is that even those without major wounding in this area cannot continue reaching if the mother figure in the exercise fails to come even a small number of times. One woman described an image of herself as a baby shaking the bars of her crib, enraged. "Where are you?"

Rita was middle-aged and working through childhood wounds left by extreme maternal deprivation when she suddenly had a vision in which she saw herself as a baby sitting on a lap of a woman who didn't exist above the waist. In her mind she was railing, *How could you do this to a baby?* This is a potent image. This is how the emotionally absent mother feels to a child: like someone who doesn't really exist. It is a shock, a threat to survival, and therefore a trauma to the child's nervous system.

### The need for Mother's physical presence

Infants and young children absolutely require the physical presence of a caretaker. Without a caretaker, a baby can't survive. Without a caretaker present, there's no chance for the essential needs detailed in chapter 2 to be provided.

Just as there are many reasons behind a mother's emotional absence, there are many reasons a mother may be physically absent. Absences that are too early or too long or too frequent will of course leave marks. A mother can't be emotionally present if she's not physically present at least part of the time.

I am not one to argue that women must be stay-at-home moms. Many mothers don't have a choice about working if they are going to feed their families, and others are enriched and fulfilled in important ways that enhance their capacities as mothers. Studies have shown that a mother's satisfaction is a key variable in determining how well her children do. A mother who stays home because she is "supposed to," even though it makes her depressed and cranky, is no asset.[50] There are also findings suggesting that for toddlers and older children, high-quality child care may support their development.[51] The greatest concern is with leaving children for long stretches during their first year when they are least able to tolerate separation. The amount of time away is also a factor. It's hard for moms to be sensitive and attuned when they are gone ten or twelve hours a day.

Apart from whatever minimal level of physical availability is needed (which varies by the child), it becomes more a matter of quality than of quantity. I have seen cases where even extraordinary levels of physical absence can be forgiven when the child is bonded to the parent and feels loved. This isn't to say there isn't a price to pay with significant physical absence, but it appears to be a lower price than that paid by many who had mothers at home most of the time. The permanent absence by death is another subject altogether and has different impacts.

Of course a child's age is a significant factor. Older children have more resources to help them tolerate Mother's absence. If they have been well cared for early, they have had more of a chance to internalize an image of a loving mother and are further along in developing a sturdy sense of self.

Unfortunately, for the undermothered, the bond is not strong, so there is generally more need for her physical presence, not less.

### What happens when Mother is not emotionally present?

Daniel Stern, MD, author of several books on the mother–infant relationship, notes that a baby is very tuned in to the energetic presence or absence of the mother. The mother is the center of the baby's world, and the baby is intensely tuned in to her feeling world. When he cannot feel his mother being emotionally present, it is distressing.

Stern's focus is the baby's experience in these situations. He describes what happens when the baby can only sense his mother "mentally hovering somewhere else. Somewhere he does not want to go. In identifying with her, he feels her emotional dullness creeping into himself."[52] In essence, a baby of a dissociated woman may follow her into the state of dissociation, sometimes taking on the mother's sense of woodenness and numbing. As one insightful adult reported from the perspective of her childhood self, "Mommy's presence props me up. When she goes away, I go away and lose contact with myself."

Understandably, it is more difficult for a child to stay present without the anchor of the mother. Sometimes the child blames herself for Mother's "going away" and concludes, "I am too much."

Researchers have identified two response patterns in infants whose mothers are emotionally absent. One is to turn away from the mother, avoiding contact with her in order to maintain a more pleasant state. Not surprisingly, children with mothers who show little emotional expression more often develop a self-sufficient attachment style.[53] The other pattern, as Stern describes, is "to make extraordinary efforts to charm his mother, to pull her along—to act as an antidepressant to her."[54] Hardly a job for a baby!

So the options seem to be to follow Mommy into the black hole of no feeling, to sever some of the connection in order to avoid the hole, or to become Mommy's rescuer. Take a moment to consider which, if any, of these, you might have done if your mother was emotionally absent. (You may have done all three at different times.)

This distress in the face of Mother's emotional blankness is supported by the "still-face" experiment. Here, the mother is instructed to suddenly wipe all expression and movement off her face while looking at her baby. This study investigated babies' responses to mothers' inexpressiveness. The experiment lasted only three minutes, but "the consistent pattern of infant behavior in the still-face situation is repeated attempt to elicit Mother's response, followed by somber expression, orientation away from Mother, and finally withdrawal. All this takes place in less than three minutes."[55] The researchers describe the babies collapsing into a self-protective state in which they later resort to techniques for self-comforting. The same pattern has been noticed in hospitalized infants. Infants depend on the stimulation they get from Mother's energetic and emotional presence.

In the still-face experiments, these previously secure babies warmed up again to their mothers and returned to their former intimate relational dance, but what happens when Mother is often remote, dazed, and inexpressive? Or what happens if the young child has experienced other trauma—say, medical trauma, or physical or sexual abuse—and has learned to dissociate? Will it be so easy to reengage then?

Citing research, author Sue Gerhardt concludes, "For a baby, the most painful experience of all seems to be not being able to get Mother's attention."[56] This seems even more unbearable than maltreatment. Mother, after all, is the baby's link to the world and the best hope for getting needs met, assuming Mother is the primary caretaker.

One common type of emotionally absent mother is the woman who is depressed. Depressed mothers are found to be less interactive with their children, and their babies show fewer positive feelings, become insecurely attached as toddlers, and do less well on cognitive tasks.[57] (Remember that the brain is largely turned on and built through social interaction.) The stress will also lead to a more sensitive gastrointestinal and autonomic nervous systems and inability or unwillingness to interact socially with an adult trying to establish contact.[58] Such children often grow into adults who are not used to warm, nourishing contact and still need to learn how to establish what they should have had as babies.

The depressed mother's face is too like the still-face experiment. An absence of nonverbal signals deprives the child of support and direction. Even something as simple as a smile (that is genuine) has tremendous power to cheer on the toddler taking his first steps, to communicate safety and acceptance, and engage the child in relationship. How else does the young child know that Mommy is okay? In a similar way, a look of surprise or disapproval helps a child orient to his environment. Mother's responses are an important help in navigating the world.

The emotionally absent mother is not present to provide many of the functions of the Good Mother, but perhaps most important is that her heart is not available to the child. She doesn't create a real bond with her child. While other types of mothers may do a poor job of providing some of the Good Mother functions such as guidance, encouragement, and protection, some do create a bond. The needy mother, for example, creates a connection heavily influenced by her needs, rather than the child's. The overcontrolling mother is often both bonded to and overidentified with her child.

## Mutual standoff

I have not seen a case in which a child (often now an adult) has turned away from a mother who is consistently turned toward the child.[59]Attachment research indicates that when a child defies the instinctive urge to want to attach to his or her mother, it is because the mother has been perceived in some important way as unavailable. My basic thesis is that children turn away from Mother out of disappointment and hurt and in self-defense. They turn away because it hurts too much to turn toward another and not be met.

Mothers, being the imperfect humans that they are, can react to perceptions and fears of being unwanted or rejected by a child. They turn away out of their own wounding. Mother and child can get into a state of mirroring each other in which both are rejecting the other, building walls in response to the other's walls or unavailability. Both tend to be emotionally disengaged from the other, except in cases where a child (or adult child) continues to contort herself, trying to win Mother's love. Because Mother is our first love and our needs are so strong during our early years, it's very hard to let go of the desire to finally win her love. Yet the more unresponsive Mother was, the earlier we tend to give up, as seen in the self-sufficient pattern.

For a year my local newspaper followed the story of a teenage girl who, with her boyfriend, planned the murder of the girl's mother, which the boyfriend then carried out. Both showed signs of being seriously sociopathic, without remorse or feeling. It was uncomfortable for me to contemplate a child being so coldhearted toward her own mother, although I am certainly aware of the rage many, if not most, of the undermothered feel. A psychologist testified that the girl had turned off her feelings as a way of coping with the severe neglect, verbal abuse, and occasional physical abuse she had experienced over a period of many years with her raging, alcoholic mother. She had the maturity of an eight-year-old, evaluators said. The same girl had reportedly "blossomed" earlier when living in a supportive family environment with an aunt. The story is a tragic example of the deep damage that can occur in a toxic parent-child relationship when the more normal feelings of mutual affection get distorted into a mirroring of the mutual defenses of numbing and out-of-control acting out.

Most of the time, thank heaven, it doesn't get to such extremes, but the mirroring is still evident. In the pairs of mothers and their adult children that I have seen, mothers who cared for their children out of obligation are then cared for in their elderly years by their adult children out of a similar obligation.

I have seen this dance change when either party significantly becomes more emotionally transparent and healed. More often the adult children lead the way in this after years of inner healing, although one woman described how her mother hit bottom after the loss of her spouse and dealing with recovery from serious depression. In this case the previously emotionally absent mother changed the dance by becoming more vulnerable and authentic in the relationship.

## Thirty possible reasons Mother wasn't there

- She was grieving.
- She had too many children to attend to.
- She was mentally ill.
- She was in the hospital.
- You were in the hospital.
- You were separated by circumstance (war, natural disaster, economic calamity, prison . . .).
- You started off on a bad foot and didn't bond well. Mothering felt like work to her, and this brought up internal conflict and/or shame.
- She had narcissistic wounds and was too busy attending to her own needs.
- She didn't know how to mother and avoided contact out of guilt and inadequacy.
- She was busy taking care of someone else (an ill parent, spouse . . .).
- She was overwhelmed with practical tasks, like moving the household time and time again.
- She was addicted to alcohol or drugs.

o  She was working two jobs to keep a roof over your head.

o  She was a "career woman," and this took all of her energy.

o  She was going to school (which took forever!).

o  She was too busy with her romantic and sexual liaisons.

o  She was just a child herself.

o  She was worn out, exhausted, or physically ill.

o  She was in shock (from trauma).

o  She didn't want to be there. Maybe she didn't even want to have a child.

o  She was crowded out by someone else taking over the mothering role.

o  She was a lost child herself, never bonded with her mother, and had no reference point for being an attentive, involved parent.

o  She was depressed and didn't have the emotional or mental resources.

o  She was afraid to show her love, afraid to bond with anyone.

o  She thought you had what you needed, and she was told by others to not do too much for fear of spoiling you.

o  She spent all her energy trying to protect herself from a raging or abusive partner.

o  She cut off emotionally to protect herself from the unresolved pain of her own childhood.

o  She thought she was there, but didn't have a clue about what was really needed.

o  She was emotionally numb from medication.

o  She died.

### How a child interprets Mommy's absence

Perhaps if we boil these thirty reasons down to three basic messages, what the undermothered child hears is one or more of the following:

○ I don't have it to give.

○ You ask/take too much. Your needs are too much.

○ I don't really care about you.

When children perceive that Mother simply doesn't have it to give, somewhere in their souls, they are often compassionate. One woman, Farah, told me, "I could feel that my mother was suffering and unhappy, so I tried to not ask for very much." Knowing her mother was overstressed, Farah minimized her needs as much as possible. Curiously, her mother much later commented that Farah had separated from her prematurely. How do you stay connected to someone who is rarely there? Farah said the message she received from her mother was "Don't lean on me." She was simply complying.

While in some ways the situation may seem easier when a child perceives that Mother simply doesn't have love and attention to give, it is difficult for a child to not personalize this and much harder if Mommy seems to have it to give to someone else.

In some cases, Mommy simply runs out of gas. She is often most engaged with her first child, but with three or more children, she may be just going through the motions, coping as best she can by the time her last child comes along. (Imagine nine or ten! In large families, older children often take on parenting responsibilities for the younger ones and serve as surrogate mothers.) Of course the baby in this situation doesn't know that Mother is exhausted; all he knows is that Mother isn't there.

There is a felt difference for a child between the mother who is working two jobs and coming home exhausted and the mother who is busy talking on the phone, laughing with her friends. Then it becomes, "I'm too busy *for you*. You aren't important to me."

When Mother seems stingy or withholding or burdened by having to provide, children often take away the feeling that *they* are the problem and their needs are too much. In response to this, some children will become very compliant and learn to hide or minimize their needs, as Farah did.

When it seems that Mother really could do more but just isn't motivated to, we often end up believing that she doesn't really care about us, accentuating the painful feeling that something must be wrong with us or that we are unlovable.

> ➤ How did you interpret your mother's unavailability as a child?

> ➤ What would be your more objective assessment of it now?

## When Mother is the only one there

Unfortunately, there are times when a not-so-adequate mother is the only caretaker in the home or consistently in the home. The absence of a father (or a second mother figure) makes it even harder on an undermothered child. There is no one else to go to for care, and maintaining the fragile bond with Mother becomes even more essential.

It is commonly believed that part of a father's role is to help a child separate from Mother. Whereas Mother represents the nest and the early merged relationship where the child does not yet know him- or herself as separate from Mom, Father represents the world beyond Mother and is a bridge into that larger world. Whether the relationship with Mother is satisfying or not satisfying, it's harder for a child to move beyond Mother's orbit when she is the only parent there.

### Three mothers, three messages (an exercise)

To get a sense of how powerfully various types of mothers shape a child's experience, let's play with a taste of three types of mothers: the prickly mother, the emotionally absent mother, and our archetypal Good Mother. Your first task is to cast the three characters. The following may help.

For the first character, we've all had experience with someone who is prickly, so that shouldn't be hard to imagine. Prickly people are critical, quickly irritated, and harsh. For the emotionally absent mother, think of your own if this fits, or do your best to imagine it. And for the last character, the Good Mother, you've likely experienced a nurturing person somewhere in your life that you can use as a model. If you haven't personally experienced this, you might be able to call up a loving mother you saw in a movie.

This works best as a guided imagery exercise, which requires putting yourself in a relaxed state at the beginning. You might have someone read the instructions so that you can more deeply sink into the experience. Or, you can record the instructions on a tape and play them back for yourself. It all depends on how easily you access the more relaxed states of consciousness involved. A few people can just read, close their eyes, and be there.

This exercise can bring up some strong feelings, so you might want to choose a time that allows for some reflection afterward. Certainly you'll want to make sure there won't be any interruptions in the environment, so turn off the phone, and let others know you are unavailable for half an hour at least. After each question there should be enough of a pause for your experience to unfold without feeling rushed. We'll imagine each type of mother from the perspective of three different ages, starting with the prickly mother.

Find a position in which you are comfortably supported. You can lie down if you like. Take a couple of deep breaths, feeling your body relax as you release each breath. Enjoy the sense of relaxation that comes as you give yourself this time to settle in. Allow your eyes to close gently if that is comfortable.

This is not an exercise where you need to do anything. It's a chance to relax and follow, allowing feelings, images, and sensations to come to you as you fall into a deeper and deeper state of relaxation and well-being.

We'll start with the prickly mother. Tune in to whatever feelings and image you associate with this mother. Get a good sense of her energy.

Imagine that you are lying on a blanket in a sunny nursery or room. You are about six months old, and you hear birds singing in the background. Notice the colors of the walls and blanket and the temperature in the room. Your mother comes in to feed you. How do you feel as she approaches? What is her voice like? How does she move? What is it like when she picks you up? How does she interact with you? What do you notice in your body? What happens to your breathing? *(long pause)*

Now imagine being any age between four and six years old. You're at home, playing. What are you doing? What is she doing? Does she play with you? Notice the quality of her voice, movements, and the expressions on her face. How does it feel to have her here? What do you notice in your body? Pay careful attention to your inner state right now. What thoughts, images, and sensations are you aware of? What emotions? *(long pause)*

Move forward in time to an age between eight and ten. Imagine yourself in an environment of your choosing with Mother not far away. What are you doing? How far away is Mother, and how does it feel to have her in this scene with you? Notice how it feels in your body.

Bring yourself back to the present for a moment. You might want to write down a few words to remind you of this experience.

Now we're going through the sequence with the emotionally absent mother. Take a moment to tune in to what she feels like.

First imagine yourself at six months, lying in the sunny room. This mother comes in to feed you. Notice the qualities that are present in her interactions with you and especially notice how you feel in your body and your emotions. What is this time with your mother like? *(long pause)*

Now imagine being any age between four and six years old. You're at home, playing, with Mother not far away. What are you doing? What is she doing? Does she play with you? Notice the quality of her voice, her movements, the expressions on her face. How does it feel to have her here? What do you notice in your body? Pay careful attention to your inner state. *(long pause)*

Move forward in time to an age between eight and ten. Imagine yourself in an environment of your choosing with Mother not far away. What are you doing? How far away is Mother, and how does it feel to have her in this scene with you? Notice how it feels in your body. *(pause)*

Bring yourself back to the present and write down a few words to remind you of this experience.

We'll go through one last time with the Good Mother. Put yourself back in the nursery. Hear her voice as she approaches. What sounds does she make? How does she look at you? What expression is on her face? Notice how she reaches out to touch you and what qualities are there in her movements. Notice what her touch feels like and how you feel with her. How do you feel in your body? *(long pause)*

Now imagine being any age between four and six years old. You're at home, playing. It can be anywhere you want, inside or outside, with Mother in the environment. When you want to engage her, she is there. How does she play with you? Notice the quality of her voice, movements, and the expressions on her face. How does it feel to have Mommy playing with you? What do you notice in your body? Pay careful attention to your inner state right now. *(long pause)*

Now we're going to experience one more age with the Good Mother. This time you're somewhere between eight and ten. Notice where you are and what you're doing. How far away is Mother, and how does it feel to have her in this scene with you? Notice how it feels in your body.

Bring yourself back to the present and write down a few words to remind you of this experience.

What did you notice? How did you feel being around each of these mother figures?

Often prickly mothers (and prickly people in general) cause us to tighten our muscles, hold our breath, and hold back our spontaneity. Since almost anything we do could be wrong, we're more inhibited around them. The phrase *walking on eggshells* describes how many of us feel around someone with this disposition. We often much prefer not to have them around.

In contrast, we like being around nurturing mothers. It brings out our affectionate side. We smile and feel happy, and we have lots of permission and support to try new things and to be silly.

Emotionally absent mothers often leave us feeling absent. People may feel spaced out, disconnected, and less here with this type of mother. You may have found yourself more serious and alone in the imagined scenes with her. Some find themselves angry and want to do something big to get her attention.

Is there really any question that a mother's basic disposition and energy profoundly affects her child?

## Original Loss

Author Judith Viorst in *Necessary Losses* calls the loss of the mother–child connection Original Loss. It is our first loss and tilts us in such a way that future losses will involve more risk.

"Studies show that early childhood losses make us sensitive to losses we encounter later on," writes Viorst. "And so, in mid-life, our response to a death in the family, a divorce, the loss of a job, may be a severe depression—the response of that helpless and hopeless, and angry child."[60] To the extent we've done our healing work, we're not limited to that response, but her point is an important one.

Viorst goes on to say, "Severe separations in early life leave emotional scars on the brain because they assault the essential human connection: The mother–child bond which teaches us that we are lovable. The mother–child bond that teaches us how to love. We cannot be whole human beings—indeed, we may find it hard to be human—without the sustenance of this first attachment."[61]

As we've seen, the absence of a mother who is really there for you is a huge loss, but the situation is not as hopeless as you may feel. The second half of the book outlines a number of ways we can make up for and heal this mother wound. First let's listen to the voices of some who were undermothered and hear how it was for them.

# 6.

# Voices of the Undermothered

Examining the experience of adults who were undermothered provides interesting insight into the phenomena of the emotionally absent mother and her impacts on her children. In this chapter I will share a few of the trends I found among the mothers themselves, their adult children, how they suffer and heal, and the relationships between them. Much of this information came from formal interviews I did with adults who identified as undermothered. The interviews gave me a chance to be consistent in my questioning and test out some of my concepts.

## Who was that masked woman?

Those of us of a certain age remember the Lone Ranger show on television. There was always somebody at the end of the show asking, "Who was that masked man?" The hero of the show was a one-dimensional character never seen without his mask.

Likewise for many of the undermothered, their mothers are never fully seen. Sometimes they hide out in their bedrooms. Sometimes they hide behind a still, expressionless face. Sometimes they "put on their face" and go out. In more extreme cases they are cardboard figures to their children.

Part of the healing process is taking the mask off Mother, seeing her life story and getting a picture of the forces that shaped her and the feelings that were hidden.

In my interviews with those who identified themselves as undermothered, I asked several questions about their mother's life stories. Several things struck me. One was how much these mothers were undermothered themselves. A number came from large immigrant families and were essentially lost children. They never had a close, nurturing relationship with their mothers, and they seemed to not know what was possible.

A second fact that caught my attention was how often these mothers were untreated trauma survivors or the children of trauma survivors. Some bore scars of the Holocaust. Many experienced the tragic loss of a family member, which they never got over. The not-getting-over is the critical factor here. Research indicates that a woman's ability to form a secure attachment with her child is related more to her capacity to deal with painful emotional events than it is to her actual history of trauma and loss.[62] Unfortunately, many of our mothers had little understanding or help in this arena.

A third thing that stood out was how often these women lacked independence from their spouses; usually the relationships themselves were not very nurturing. These women were hostage to their husband's needs and limitations, perhaps because they so desperately sought the love they had missed growing up. Not having a strong mother instinct or model to follow, they didn't seem to know about championing or protecting their children. Often they didn't shield children from harm inflicted by the children's fathers, whether suppressed hostility, verbal attack, or sexual abuse.

Cultural context also plays a part. Particularly before the 1970s, most women didn't perceive that it was an option to not be a mother. It was the expected life course for a woman to marry and have a family, whether this was her natural inclination or not. The result of this (then and now) is that women become mothers who are not really suited to the job. They are, as one woman put it, "reluctant mothers." They would have been more comfortable doing something else, perhaps living a career life or being a social dilettante. Caring for children wasn't "their thing."

Men could get away with this. When I was growing up, we didn't expect very much of fathers beyond financially providing for the family. If they weren't naturally suited to parenting, it was much less visible, because they were a small part of the picture. With the greatly expanded involvement of fathers in recent years, many of today's children will remember their fathers providing basic care and nurturance, along with any of the other functions of the Good Mother I described in chapter 2. This gives younger people a chance to know more dimensions of their fathers, and they are less likely in later years to ask, "Who was that masked man?" Regardless of the era, good parenting by a father has always helped make up for the holes left by an emotionally absent mother.

### Slim pickin's from Mom

Looking at my list of mothering functions, many of those I interviewed told me their mothers had fulfilled none of them. The most common exceptions were receiving some praise or encouragement and some protection.

Protection was the hardest to evaluate. Respondents several times told me that their mother protected them, but they were not able to back it up. Occasionally an interviewee could give me an example of Mother's protection, but it wasn't very often; and several times they noted that their mothers had not protected them from their father's mistreatment. Some mothers provided the usual supervision (a form of protection) we would expect from a parent, but I was often stunned by the lack of supervision. (See "Is anyone watching? Does anyone care?" on p. 101.)

When praise and encouragement were present, it was usually qualified. These children were praised for what the mothers valued (most often school achievement) but seldom celebrated and praised for themselves. The immature mother often doesn't notice and appreciate what is different from her. Such mothers reward their children when they are like them or conform to their idea of what children should be, but they don't actively support the child's own unique self. Some of those I interviewed reported receiving encouragement, but not support and not help that was tailored to their needs.

Mirroring is rare for emotionally absent mothers, leaving children without a positive self-image or clear sense of self and, by default, feeling inadequate on a deep level. Some felt belittled and shamed, although I was trying to exclude mothers who were actively negating. A child doesn't need to be belittled to end up stunted. One woman lamented that her mother had never told her that she was pretty or smart or valuable. A mother is a very important mirror for a child, and the absence of these mirroring messages can leave a child filled with self-doubt.

These mothers were also unschooled in dealing with emotion and generally had no tolerance for it. They didn't know how to deal with their children's tears, sometimes even saying aggressive things like "Stop crying or I'll give you something to cry about!" Other times the children were not directly shamed for showing their feelings, but their emotions were ignored, and they got positive attention for holding in any sad or "weak" feelings.

These remote mothers were most often remembered as most attentive during times the child was sick, although many had no memory of being touched or held at such times. For some, Mother was simply a worried face at the door.

Compared with our picture of ideal mothering, there was little that the undermothered received. Like looking at empty cupboards, it was slim pickin's.

## Lack of mentoring

Another key role almost entirely missing for the undermothered is guidance. One of the jobs of the Good Mother is to teach a child how to negotiate tasks that are challenging and somewhat beyond the child's current abilities. The Good Mother helps the child assess what he or she can handle, what is maybe a little too much, and how to back off from that; she calibrates the task to the child's abilities. When we don't get this (and haven't since learned it by other means), we're often left not knowing how to navigate life. One response is to collapse in the face of a challenging task and not try. Another is to plunge into something without the preparation or respect for our limits that would be more self-caring.

Imagine how a skilled mother helps her children plan what to pack for summer camp or how many courses at school to take without overburdening themselves. The Good Mother teaches the child how to modulate difficulty, taking into account needs and limitations (such as tiredness, stress, hunger). When we bite off more than we can chew, the Good Mother says, "That's too much, honey. Let's make it a little easier."

What I am describing is really a combination of the roles of Mother as Mentor (providing calibrated help) and Mother as Modulator (ensuring the child doesn't get overwhelmed). When we get enough of this as a child or we learn to mother ourselves, we ask, "How big a step is the right size for me? What's too big?" We recognize what we need in order to be able to take a bigger step.

One woman reported that her mother had shown her a few things like how to make salads and wash the dishes, but had taught her nothing about how to "do life"—how to have a conversation or relate to other people, how to manage her emotions, or anything important. Such mothers seem to have vacated the mentor role, or at the least to feel quite insecure in it.

Another interviewee described how it seemed his mother didn't mind being a sounding board on occasion, but she seemed reticent to get involved otherwise, perhaps afraid to pry. She never put out a welcome mat, inviting her children to come to her with problems or needs. It is the mother's responsibility to build the foundation for this. Children can't be expected to intuit when it's okay to ask Mother for help.

## Missed connections

One of the questions I asked in my interviews was, "If you could give your mother one quality that was missing, what would it be?" Most often the answer had something to do with the ability to make an emotional connection. Generally it was connection to them as a child that felt missing, but some acknowledged that their mothers didn't seem to make emotional connections with anybody.

More often than not, the adults I interviewed had no memories of close times with their mothers as children. No memories of being held, looked at with loving eyes, or emotionally met during important moments.

To be emotionally met is to have others touch your experience in such a way that you know they get it. They know what you've been through and what it means to you. Generally how we know this is through responses that demonstrate empathy or mirroring. It's not possible for others to know our experience precisely, but we want them to at least try. We want them to care about our experience. When we're brushed off or discounted or told that we feel something other than we actually do feel, it leaves us feeling isolated and alone.

Carol described an incident that happened when she was six. Her life was actually endangered for a few moments, and she successfully negotiated this. When Carol told her mother about it, her mother dismissed the danger and acted as if the account was implausible, thereby missing a very important moment in Carol's life. It was a moment when she could so easily have given a Good Mother message like, "You were so smart and so brave, and I'm so glad you're here." It could have been a moment when Carol felt cherished and knew she was loved. Instead, it left her with the feeling that she couldn't trust her mother to be there for her.

These nonconnecting mothers are not good communicators. Not only do they miss opportunities like the one just cited, but they fail to respond to overtures made. One woman put a self-disclosing letter under her mother's pillow as a teen, hoping to open up some level of communication, but her mother never mentioned it.

For those who feel well loved, it may be astounding to hear that people can go through their entire childhoods and not have a single memory of closeness and connection, yet I saw this in a significant share of the adults I interviewed. What makes it so hard to imagine is that it flies right in the face of our collective image of what a mother is supposed to be.

## The mechanical mom

The picture we get of mothers who are emotionally absent is one of a woman who seems not quite fully human. One man said his parents were like statues to him; they didn't feel like real human beings. Others have spoken of not being able to find a human heart in there and feeling as if Mother was "not real."

Alma told me she remembers her mother as a person, remembers that her mother was there, but has absolutely no memory of interacting with her. Alma felt like a nonperson to her mother, as if she didn't exist. She felt more at home in the tree house in the backyard than with her mother. I suggest this is the result of a mother who brought no sense of realness to their interactions.

Many of these mothers were quite checked out, living in their own world. This condition was not always ongoing, but might be present for a period of years. I suspect this coincides with unresolved trauma, grief, and depression.

Certainly if a mother is emotionally absent, it will be impossible for her to attune to her child's needs. I am speaking here both of a particular child's needs and of children's needs in general. I have previously listed some of the aspects inherent in being a child—being undeveloped and without mastery, having limited capacities, being dependent, needing lots of affection and holding, and needing protection, guidance, and mentoring, among others. I found that the experiential world of the child was totally lost to these "mechanical moms." These parents (and it was usually both) seemed more comfortable seeing their children as little adults than responding to them as children. Children were not allowed to be loud, exuberant, or messy, and their bids for closeness were pretty consistently rejected.

Sometimes Mother is obviously out of commission. More insidious are the cases where she looks like the desirable mother, does many of the outward things that she believes constitute the central role of the mother, but is experienced by her children as not really there and not attuned. Some of these mothers may even think of themselves as happily settled into mothering. It's just that they define it so differently! Their focus is on making sure the children are clothed and educated and that family conflicts stay out of sight.

In some homes there is pressure to maintain the illusion of a happy family. In one case, the father repeatedly told the children what a wonderful mother they had. The mother, incidentally, spent most of her time in her bedroom, forcing herself out to participate in important holiday celebrations, times when it was most important to prop up such a picture.

Children of such mothers often grow up intellectually believing they were loved but not *feeling* loved. Especially if mothers make an effort to do some child-oriented things like go to parent–teacher conferences and throw a birthday party once in a while, it can be confusing. Because children have nowhere else to go and are dependent on their parents, they will often push out of consciousness any feelings of not being loved. The feelings erupt later when the adult is in therapy or struggling with self-esteem or relationship issues.

A few of these mothers learned to connect later in life, although most did not. One mother first told her daughter (now middle-aged) that she loved her after reading in a Dear Abby column that this is something mothers should say to their children.

As might be expected, these emotionally distant mothers did not touch their children much, leading to a strong touch hunger or the opposite, touch aversion. One woman said she had to learn to touch others, because it didn't come naturally to her.

Often with these touch-avoidant mothers, touch enters the relationship when the mothers are aged and the now-healed children initiate more warmth. Sometimes the mothers start reaching out when they are widowed, lonely, and need more support themselves. It is often in their advanced years that the mechanical mom finally becomes human.

## Is anyone watching? Does anyone care?

The picture that emerges of many of these parents is one of extreme disengagement. Both mother and father are missing in action.

One of the ways this shows up is in a marked lack of supervision. I heard of children wandering on their own outside the home as young as two and often by three or four. They are walking home alone from school or from the corner store at five and often sent to do things on their own at an age that most today would consider totally inappropriate or dangerous. When the dentist of an eight-year-old called the child's mother, the mother thought the child must have misbehaved. She couldn't imagine that sending a child that age to a dentist alone was inappropriate.

Some disengaged parents don't seem to care or want to know what their children are doing. When one adolescent boy told his mother where he was going or what he was going to do, she would reply, "I don't care."

Some children, especially by adolescence, like the freedom of not having anyone to answer to, but this comes with a price. Children and adolescents often have not yet developed the judgment that would lead to wise choices, and not having parameters on their behavior feels like no one really cares. When Bobby fell off his bicycle and had to have stitches, his mother grounded Bobby for a short while, limiting him to the backyard. He noticed that he actually felt happy about this, because for the first time it felt that his mother was watching out for him.

In some households there was virtually no conversation in the family. There was a minimal amount of functional communication, but no discussion of the child's activities or friends. Contrast this with parents who talk with their children about essentially every part of their kids' lives, who know their children's ups and downs, hopes and fears, and who support them where they lack confidence and celebrate even their smallest successes.

The lack of involvement described in this section is neglect. It's not the neglect of children going without food or shelter, but it's still neglect. The scars caused by such lack of involvement and emotional nurture are significant. Homes without toys, children never related to as children, children who are strangers to their parents—these are serious failings.

Living with a disengaged mother, especially if coupled with a disengaged father, is almost like living on your own as a child.

> In what areas of your life was your mother engaged, and where was she disengaged?

> If you had a father in the home, did he mirror this or have a different pattern?

## Clueless

I found these emotionally absent mothers singularly unreflective, clueless about any role they may have played in their children's early or later problems.

When a middle-aged woman recently shared with her mother how difficult her childhood had been for her, the mother responded, "If we'd known how unhappy you were as a child, we could have put you on medication." While this might show a small sense of advocacy and caring and does reflect our dominant culture's orientation toward mental health problems, it totally misses the fact that perhaps what was needed was more demonstration of love (or any of the other Good Mother roles). I think such mothers miss this fact because in their own minds they do love their children. They just don't know how to show it in a way that children really get it.

## No place to go for help

We all know that bad things sometimes happen in the world, but for the world to feel like a place we want to be, we also need to believe that there are places we can go for help; that when we are on our knees begging for our life, there will be a drop of kindness. A child, who is by nature dependent, needs someone to turn to, someone who is safe, someone with the power to help.

In "Mother as Home Base" (p. 40), I described Mother as the place where we can always go for shelter, help, and comfort.

This is clearly not the case for the undermothered. None of the people I interviewed could recall a time when they went to their mother for help and received a satisfying response. Most learned early not to ask. One man recalled how anytime he went to his mother with a request as a child, she would counter with, "What do you need that for?" Children of such mothers often feel that asking for help will get them in trouble. The feeling is that their mothers don't want to be bothered.

I noticed a disturbing pattern of mothers being unable to respond to direct pleas for assistance even when the children were grown. A notable number of the undermothered whom I interviewed reached a point in their early adult years where their mental health failed and they needed help. Naomi was visiting at her mother's when her psychiatrist phoned her. When Naomi finished the call and told her mother, "I'm very depressed. I need help!" her mother replied, "You don't need help. All you need is a hot bath." Another mother, confronted by her twenty-two-year-old son sharing that he was seeing a psychiatrist, simply walked out of the room without a word.

Margaret asked her parents if she could live with them when her young husband was hospitalized and their situation terribly unstable and stressful. Her parents refused her request, which led to years of strained distance between them and Margaret's decision to never go to them for help again.

So, unfortunately, we see mothers minimizing their children's problems, mothers denying significant problems happening right under their noses, mothers shaming and blaming their children for having problems, and we even find mothers expressing indignant anger when children *don't* come to them with a problem, as we'll see next.

When Sharon's mother discovered that Sharon had undergone an abortion and not told her about it, she confronted her fifteen-year-old daughter. Perhaps she felt hurt, perhaps insulted; her behavior was angry. What she failed to communicate was caring about Sharon. She didn't ask how and why this had happened or why Sharon didn't feel comfortable sharing it with her, although she was obviously upset with the fact that Sharon hadn't come to her. Rather than being a time when Sharon could at last feel some support, she simply felt in trouble with her mom.

The foundation for children knowing they can come to their mothers with needs and problems is established early—as is the sense that mothers either don't want to know, don't have time and energy to deal, or aren't much help. By the time a child becomes an adolescent, trying to reach him or her during periods of significant stress is often a case of too little, too late.

> ➤ Did you go to your mother for help in times of significant need? How did she respond? How did this affect your relationship?

> ➤ Would you go to her for help now (if she's still alive)? If not, why not?

A mother's failure to provide a home base, a place to return to, a place that's safe, sets a person up for feeling like a motherless child.

## Feeling like a motherless child

The undermothered often feel as if they don't really have a mother—although they do, which complicates the picture. The feeling is of being motherless, but the actuality is that someone is there, whom the world recognizes as one's mother. How to reconcile the feeling of being motherless with the actuality is part of the challenge of the undermothered adult child. To dismiss the feeling is to continue to abandon the child. Much of healing is learning to respond to that feeling.

A term sometimes used to describe this is *orphan complex* or *orphan archetype*. It is the feeling of being without parents and without love. This feeling is often deeply repressed because it is so painful; to be without these things threatens a child's survival. One adult described opening up to the long-repressed feeling, *I could die for want of love.*

In writing about the orphan archetype, Jungian analyst Rose-Emily Rothenberg notes a pervasive feeling of unworthiness and a felt need for support. "He [the orphan] feels that he is the 'injured one' and needs all the care he can possibly get." [63] She describes a pattern of dependency and clinging to whatever and whoever represents the protection and security of the mother.

One way this shows up is in a kind of love hunger that causes people to stay in relationships that are abusive or unsatisfying, because the feeling of need is so desperate that the individual can't leave. Not having an internal reference point for being well loved, they often feel, *This is better than nothing.* Others find it easier (and more familiar) to go without love than to go near that wound.

This need for nurturing goes beyond partnership and can be as subtle as finding it difficult to turn away from anyone offering any kind of positive attention. For years I found that if someone did something nice for me, I felt bound to them. Slowly, I realized that emotional nurturance is not such a rare thing and that I can decide in each relationship when I want to turn elsewhere. One act of kindness isn't a life contract.

Others who are emotionally starved fixate on food, attempting to use physical nourishment to stand in for emotional nourishment. Perhaps because it never does and never can, the satisfaction is never complete. One woman who knows that she goes to food to feed her emotional hunger or when she is stressed suggested that emotional starvation is behind our obesity epidemic. Many of the undermothered have histories of eating disorders and binge eating.

Here are some questions to help you explore this.

➤ Have you ever felt "like a motherless child"?

➤ How does your love hunger show up?

➤ How might you cover up your hunger for love, support, and protection?

## No mother, no self

When I was brainstorming titles for this book, I made a play on words on the title of a well-known book by Nancy Friday called *My Mother, My Self.* On the most basic level, it is simple: *No Mother, No Self.*

Our relationship with our mothers has a big impact on how we experience our self as a child. A child with a critical parent often internalizes the judgment and is riddled with self-doubt, inadequacy, and shame. But with a neglectful parent, an emotionally flat or absent parent, there isn't enough mirroring and support for a child's fragile self to fully develop.

This is different from low self-esteem, where there may be a quite definite picture and experience of self that is weighed down by doubt and shame. Here the experience of self is itself indefinite, not fully formed. One woman complained that she had no sense of "me." Another told me that her mother didn't have a clear sense of self, "and rather than feel she gave me a sense of self, it was more like she sucked mine out of me."

Blank begets blank, absence begets absence. No mother, no self.

Perhaps the positive side of this is that unlike those who are identified with Mother and fail to individuate from her, thus shadowing her their entire lives, those without this connection—if they do the psychological work necessary—are freer to fashion a self that is more of their own making.

## No anchor

The sense of self and of Mother are important anchors in our lives. Without them, we can feel disconnected, lost, and ungrounded in the world. This is sometimes reflected in images of floating in a dark space, like an astronaut whose connecting cord is broken. Others describe it as drifting at sea, like a piece of flotsam. This feeling is often carried throughout life, unless efforts are made to change the situation.

This lack of anchor and of ground has many implications. It affects our relationships with both the world and our bodies. When it affects our relationship with the world, we might drift through life, never part of any community and never solidly connected to anyone. One strongly spiritually oriented woman told me that without Mother to anchor her to the world, she felt as if she never fully came in to this dimension.

Disconnection from the body can begin very early. When a baby is nursed by a mother who isn't really present, the child has nothing to anchor to, no sense of ground, and loses her own connection with her body. (Recall the child following Mother into dissociative states described earlier.) If you are not tuned in to your body, you don't know when you're hungry and when you're full. You don't know what your body wants or needs because you're not really there. This contributes to eating disorders as well as to accidents and illnesses.

## Common challenges of the undermothered

The problems experienced by the undermothered come as no surprise. They relate quite clearly to the missing functions of the Good Mother. Here is a list of fifteen common problems I found.

## Holes in your sense of value and self-esteem

The undermothered, as children, did not feel valued and especially did not feel seen. They were not mirrored and received very little support or encouragement. Most often, they did not feel loved. Is it any surprise, then, that as adults their sense of self doesn't come out shining?

## Feeling as if you don't have enough support

Not having gotten much support as children leaves the undermothered with a less confident sense of self and less inner support because there wasn't a Good Mother to internalize. This lack of felt support often shows up as insecurity and difficulty moving ahead. Those who have become particularly self-sufficient sometimes don't feel this lack because they've learned to soldier through on their own; yet with the right push, the defense breaks down and the need is exposed.

## Difficulty accepting and advocating for your needs

In general, *need* is a dirty word for the undermothered, because needs are associated with the painful memory of having needs that were not met or the perception of Mother turning away from you because of your needs. Needs often have become a source of shame and something to hide. You can't advocate for your needs unless you feel some right to have them and some expectation that others will be responsive. Some find it almost impossible to ask for help.

## Feeling undernourished and emotionally starved

A number of those I interviewed underscored this as one of their biggest challenges. They felt like they were still trying to make up for the affection they missed as children. (See "Feeling like a motherless child," p. 105)

## Difficulty taking in love and establishing intimate relationships

Although the undermothered often feel starved for love, this doesn't make it easy to take in. Often there is heightened tension around this need and some armoring. Being intimate requires being vulnerable and showing needs and feelings. Especially those with a more self-sufficient, avoidant attachment style have difficulty with this.

The undermothered also have less of a reference point for close relationships and less expectation of having their needs met. It's hard to trust that someone will really be there for you when this wasn't the case in that first, most formative relationship. Many also feel undeserving (sometimes this is unconscious), believing that if they were indeed deserving, Mother would have been there for them.

Those with a more dependent style may not only scare people away with their clinging behaviors but also become angry when their partners do not provide the perfect love they still seek. Their anger pushes others away, re-creating the pattern of their original loss.

## Loneliness and feelings of not belonging

There's a sort of outsider complex that comes from not feeling like a treasured part of a family. It can leave you longing to be part of something (some group or community), yet deeply ambivalent and uncomfortable putting yourself in that situation again. Many wonder if there is a place for them in this world.

One woman, who was a first child and an unplanned pregnancy, said she always felt like an intrusion in her parents' life; later when they consciously conceived and had more children, those children and the two parents seemed like a unit that she was never fully part of. Feeling unloved as a child sets the stage for chronic loneliness.

## Not knowing how to process feelings

When feelings are not shown in the childhood home (or only by an out-of-control parent) and when Mother has not helped her child learn to regulate or to name and communicate feelings, it creates a hole in an important part of life. For many, learning to identify feelings rather than act out through addictive behaviors has been a major therapeutic task; those who have kept feelings at bay need to learn how to let an emotion rise and cycle through.

## A pervasive sense of scarcity

Not all of the undermothered I spoke with suffered from a sense of scarcity, but a number of them did. Deprivation can be so deeply branded into your consciousness that it becomes a lens through which you experience life. You may feel as if there's never enough money, never enough love, and never enough joy.

Often this is complicated by discomfort around receiving. If your mother was Scrooge-like in her psychology and didn't give generously, often a part of your psyche has this same filter and doesn't give or receive in a gracious way. You then continue the legacy of scarcity.

## Sense of struggle

For many of the undermothered, life has felt hard. There has been struggle around livelihood, struggle around relationships, struggle simply to feel okay. This struggling is a different octave of the failure-to-thrive syndrome identified in orphanages.

## Depression

A very common entry point for therapy for the undermothered is seeking help for depression. Depression has a lot to do with loss, deprivation, needs not being met, not enough love, battered self-esteem, undigested pain and disappointment, grief, and lack of support.

Depression was a pretty universal experience of the undermothered I interviewed, often beginning around junior high school age or by early adulthood. A significant proportion of them had brothers or sisters who made suicide attempts, several of which were successful. Some had been suicidal themselves.

### Addictive behaviors

We live in a culture filled with addictions, so it is no surprise to find addictions among the undermothered as well. Addiction is a common response to childhood pain that has not been metabolized. It is also related to not being able to self-soothe and regulate your emotions and states of activation. Food-related addictions seem especially common to those who were emotionally undernourished.

### Feeling disempowered

Not feeling empowered is the natural result of a number of items on this list, especially the first three. Without a strong sense of self-esteem, without strong internal support, and without a healthy entitlement around needs, it's hard to feel empowered. In addition, if Mother didn't champion you during the exploration stage and didn't guide and praise your growing competence, your sense of efficacy can be seriously compromised.

Yet it starts even before this. Your first task as a baby is to get Mother to come. When Mother is not responsive to your cries, it creates a very deep sense of futility. An underresponsive mother can thus deeply hamper your sense of being able to affect your environment.

## Not feeling safe

Often the undermothered had to fend for themselves, many times in situations that were not safe. When Mother isn't there to protect you as a child, it often sets into the nervous system a pattern of hypervigilance. Insecure attachment will also lead to feeling less safe (since attachment is the primary vehicle for providing safety to the young child); and without having internalized the warm, comforting presence of the Good Mother, there isn't a reservoir of feelings of safety or security.

## Perfectionism and self-criticism

When Mother doesn't give love or praise easily, children often go to great lengths to conform to what they think Mother wants. They monitor themselves carefully and create high standards they hold themselves to. Many continue this practice throughout adulthood. In an interesting twist, this is often paired with being an underachiever rather than an overachiever. People who need to do everything well don't have permission to fail or to try new things that require a learning curve, and so they stop themselves before they begin.

## Difficulty finding your authentic voice and following your passion

Without a champion or a cheerleader, without mirroring, without unconditional acceptance, it's much harder to find your authentic self-expression. Neglect can be a setup for a lost self and lost life.

### What helps

While you can never go back to being a baby and get the holding you missed, there is much that you can do to make up for insufficient mothering. In the next chapter we'll look at the overall process of healing mother wounds, and in the remaining five chapters consider a variety of things that can help.

This variety is important because there isn't going to be one way that works for everyone; our needs are different, and we're different. For those I interviewed for this book, many things were helpful in filling the hole where Mother should have been. Here is a brief summary.

- Having others stand in for the missing mother and provide some of what she could not makes an incredible difference to children. These may include godparents, grandparents, older siblings, aunts, teachers, coaches, and other mentors. Sometimes these people provide guidance, sometimes affection, sometimes belonging. Others may protect, champion, or even supervise neglected children. For teens and adults, friendship groups and intimate partners provide some of these functions, and a number of people find that when they marry, they acquire not only a mate but also loving parents. Allowing yourself to receive nourishment from others is an essential part of healing.

- The people I interviewed had spent a lot of hours in therapy. One woman reported she'd had five therapists before the age of thirty. Many had been in therapy for ten to twenty years. Counselors not only gave them skills and helped them deal with their pain but also provided some of the care and guidance that had been missing. The re-parenting that can happen in a therapeutic relationship involves a number of complex issues that will be covered in chapter 8 on psychotherapy. A broad range of therapies can be useful.

- In addition to formal therapy, many found other kinds of groups and interventions helpful. These included spiritual and self-help groups. Books were also important.

🍐 To feel seen and heard somewhere is often huge for those who were undermothered and undermirrored. This can come in many ways and is generally paired with unconditional acceptance. To be seen and accepted as you are is part of what supports development. One woman said, "What we really want is to be seen through the eyes of love."

🍐 Caring touch often brings the warmth that has been longed for. There are many situations where safe touch is available—more than we generally imagine. Consider various forms of dance, interactive movement, athletics, massage or bodywork, and of course hugs! If you want to be more comfortable touching others, you might take as a model someone who touches easily and naturally, as often it's more a matter of permission than anything else. Taking on child care responsibilities or playing with children also affords opportunities, although we need to make sure we're not imposing an agenda but rather responding to the child. This is true of other types of caregiving, too, as with the elderly and sick and those who are grieving.

🍐 Activities that help with self-regulation were also a plus. Touch helps calm the nervous system, as do activities like yoga and meditation, being in wilderness places, or walking in serene settings.

🍐 Not everyone was receptive to inner child work, but generally those who'd experienced it found it helpful. A few came to it on their own, intuitively.

🍐 Becoming parents and nurturing their children was healing for most and pivotal for some. Of course this was paired with having done their own healing work.

Without this, we tend to repeat the dysfunctional patterns of our own upbringing. But if you've at least done your grief work, you've loosened the grip of the past and are freer to try a different way. Mothering a child can reverberate inside, where it also reaches your inner child. Of course you don't have to be a parent to be in a position to guide and nurture children, so there are opportunities for nonparents as well.

Knowing what we do now about the deficits of the undermothered and what was missing, let's turn now to healing.

# 7.

# Healing Mother Wounds

As we turn to the task of healing, we begin with an overview. In this chapter, we look at how we protect ourselves from our deepest hurts and how we need to uncover them in order to drain away the stored emotions and begin the process of recovery. We'll also talk about journaling as a place to do some of this feeling work, and look at the thorny emotion of anger, which we so often avoid—especially in our relationship with Mother.

## The cover-up

It is probably apparent to you that you or someone you care about has a "mother wound." You may be surprised that some adults who suffer significantly from mother wounds are unaware and deny them completely. Therapists recognize that many times those with the most wounding have created the biggest cover-ups to hide the damage from view. Clients may go so far as to idealize their parents, as if to create a monument that cannot be questioned.

Unfortunately, that's what it is—a monument, a bigger-than-life story. But denial is never foolproof, and there will often be clues that something was amiss in the mother–child relationship. In addition to the problems listed at the end of the last chapter, more immediate clues include the following:

- When you see a tender mother–child interaction, you are emotionally triggered. You may feel choked up and teary or push away the pain by becoming critical and dismissive. (It hurts to see what you didn't have.)

- You would just as soon not look deeply into your relationship with your mother. Better to "let sleeping dogs lie."

- When you visit your mother, you find yourself numbing or going into a trance state in which you are not fully present. Visits are always upsetting, and you find yourself back in painful childhood feelings.

- You crave true closeness yet feel uncomfortable and afraid of it. It is unfamiliar to you.

- You feel some core shame and suffer from feelings (often hidden) that there is something unlovable about you.

- You avoid having children of your own, feeling somehow not quite like "parent material."

There are many ways we stay out of contact with our deeper feelings: We make keep ourselves busy, with no time to drop into feelings; stay caught in thinking (obsessions can be very useful); tense our bodies, blocking the physiological counterparts of emotions; and breathe shallowly to minimize and contain experience.

### Discovering the wound

Creating some kind of protection is natural for the places where we hurt, and it may take some time to uncover what is beneath it.

Sometimes it is life circumstances that bring the wound to the forefront. One of the most powerful of these is being left by a partner as an adult. It brings up the hole of someone not being there to love and support you, and you may experience a sense of abandonment similar to what you felt as a child. This can happen whether the partner chose to leave or died. Unresolved feelings about your mother may also be prompted by situations that have to do with mothering, such as having a child yourself or the loss that comes when your last child leaves home. Other times Mother growing old and wanting your help may be the prompt.

You may begin with noting that your relationship with your mother doesn't feel simple to you. If you are still merged with her on some level, it will feel sticky and have the feelings in it that you associate with your mother. If she seemed heavy and depressed, for example, you may feel some of that when thinking about the relationship and find it difficult to see her objectively.

Often it will take considerable time in therapy for someone with significant mother wounds to really begin to tell the truth about their childhood. There's a considerable distance between the story that one tells at first and the lived experience, and it is the lived experience, stored in the unconscious, that takes time to get to. As this is unearthed, the story that was constructed to protect the wound slowly crumbles.

Even for those who are quite aware that their relationships with their mothers somehow fall short, opening to the full depth of what was missing is likely to be resisted and happens only slowly over time. Because the wound is so painful, we naturally shy away from it. We become less sensitized only as some of the pain is carefully drained away.

## Reframing "defects" as deficits

Although the undermothered often have some sense that there was something they missed and that this "something" affects them yet today, we seldom see the correlations in a direct way.

It is my hope that the early chapters in this book have helped you make connections between what was missing in your early environment and the difficulties you struggle with now. One of the benefits readers most appreciated in my book *Healing from Trauma* was that in knowing how their symptoms related to trauma, they could stop blaming themselves. In a similar way, knowing how dissatisfactions and limitations in your life relate to mother wounds can help you realize that these are the natural result of certain conditions. Just as a plant grown in soil depleted of minerals will show certain weaknesses, a person who has not had enough nurturance, support, mirroring, and other essential nutrients will be underdeveloped in certain ways. In the language of John Bradshaw, your "defects" can then be recognized as "deficits," things you missed.

### Working through your feelings

Most fields of psychotherapy and programs like the twelve-step recovery movement hold to the notion that you can't heal what you can't feel. Numbing and cover-ups protect the wound but prevent the healing.

When we finally break through our self-protections and connect with the lived experience of our childhood, it hurts. There is a well of grief that we haven't wanted to touch. This well contains both the feelings that were too painful to experience at the time and have been stored in "encapsulated form" somewhere in our systems and the grief we feel now when we recognize what we went through and how very much we missed. Those tears we shed when we watched the movie of the child with the loving mother are grief spilling out about what might—and should—have been.

Bradshaw calls this *original pain work*. "Original pain work involves actually experiencing the original repressed feelings. I call it the uncovery process. It is the only thing that will bring about 'second-order change,' the kind of deep change that truly resolves feelings." [64]

Original pain work involves a large number of feelings to work through, including shock, anger, loneliness, fear, shame, confusion, and raw, undifferentiated pain. It also involves grief, but grief is only part of the story.

We need support and tools for this leg of the journey. We usually scoot away from our pain when we can, so the presence of caring or facilitating others may be needed to provide the support needed to do this work. I think individual psychotherapy is probably the best container for it, but it is not the only one. Group therapy, support groups, workshops, and loving relationships may all provide help.

One of my interviewees described a long grieving process with endless tears. She felt the pain and cried, but she didn't have specific memories, which is often the case with preverbal experience. Events can touch us deeply, in indelible ways, even though they are not stored in a way we can get to. Revealing this pain to another and having it touch another (unlike her mother, whose heart could not be touched) was very healing for her.

Although it may feel like the pain could go on forever, it won't. Not if you can stay present with it. When emotions of any kind are contacted (felt) in a genuine way, they change.

It also helps if you can take a half step back, disengaging enough that you can notice the process and not just be glued to the feelings. This takes you out of identification with content and into a part of yourself that is aware but not involved, often called the "witness." This can provide you with some emotional distance to help in exploring difficult feelings.

One time I was working with the pain that I had consistently felt in my heart when a certain mother wound was touched. It wasn't at root a physical pain, but I felt it physically. I was sobbing deeply. I noticed that it actually hurt less when I let the pain out than when I tried to contain it. I took this half step back when it occurred to me to feel the pain as a stream of energy pouring out of my heart. I watched as the stream, which I envisioned as a large rivulet of water, went from murky to clear and took on different color tones. I was surprised when the streaming came to an end. There were a few last gurgles and then the hole dried up. It was a long time before the pain came back.

## Journaling

Journaling is a safe place for your feelings while going through original pain work. You don't want to wear out your friends, and your therapist (if you have one) is not always available. Researchers have recognized that expressing feelings on paper (like expressing them verbally) is helpful, whereas holding in feelings is correlated with higher stress levels and disease. The journal can serve as confidant, mirror, and guide. In your journal, you are safe from judgment and criticism, and with advanced techniques like dialogues, you can learn to comfort and support yourself.

### Writing your pain

Since your journal is your confidant and a place to heal old wounds, it is an appropriate place to express your pain. It may be the pain of grief, disappointment, loss, victimization, betrayal—anything that hurts you. You honor the journal by sharing your pain, and your journal honors you by accepting it.

Writing your feelings may bring tears, and this is fine. You can make a short, parenthetical note in the journal that you are crying as you write a particular passage, which later helps you identify what exactly seems to elicit the most feeling. Obviously you want to be in a safe place to do this work, and it is helpful to have tissues and perhaps some comfort objects around you.

I find that often the tears mark a turning point. The tears show me that I have hit "pay dirt" (the real stuff), and continuing to write through them helps open my heart, which is then there as a resource for me. The open heart, with its compassion, is perhaps the most important resource we have for working with our pain.

Although we may feel like we could cry forever, it's usually a fairly limited time as measured by the clock. And in terms of intensity, we generally can handle a lot more pain than we give ourselves credit for. Avoiding pain seems so reflexive that we rarely test our capacities.

Know that you can take a break when you need to. You can lay down your journal and do something else for a while. You might choose to think about a pleasant memory (for example, a memory of someone who really cares about you). What we often call distraction may be the mind's natural way of trying to give us a breather.

You can dialogue in the journal between two parts of yourself—for example, between a part of you that is feeling the pain and an inner representation of someone who is receiving your pain (such as your therapist, if you have one) or with a wisdom figure who is outside that pain. In writing dialogues, you simply go back and forth expressing different aspects of something, usually starting on a new line each time you switch voices.

When you are writing in your journal, you're no longer alone with your pain. You are much more alone when you are holding your feelings inside.

### The healing power of anger

John Bradshaw says, "It's okay to be angry, even if what was done to you was unintentional. In fact, you *have* to be angry if you want to heal your wounded inner child." [65]

It can feel hard to be angry at your mother, the woman who gave you birth and bandaged your scraped knees. It's especially hard to feel angry when you believe that she *tried* or that she did love you—even if she was not able to show it in a way that you could feel. It's important to remember that anger isn't the goal or where you will necessarily stay forever; it's simply part of the healing process.

The origin of this anger is likely very early, as is the habit of turning off anger. The attachment theory pioneer John Bowlby said that anger is a natural response to a child's attachment needs not being met. When a child feels that anger will only lead to more distancing on Mom's part, the child learns to turn it off. Here again the two primary insecure attachment styles come into play. Those with an avoidant, self-sufficient style are most likely to repress or hide their anger and to believe it can only hurt a relationship, whereas those with the more ambivalent, preoccupied style have learned to sometimes use their anger to get another's attention.

Beginning in childhood but continuing into adulthood, we may use anger to help us push off and separate from another. Anger therefore has a positive developmental role to play. It is part of coming to your own experience, which sometimes differs from the family myth. Now as an adult, anger comes when you say, "This was my experience, and what I got was not enough." If that seems a little too strong, consider, "This is my experience. I have angry feelings left over from being a child and feeling frustrated when I didn't get what I felt I needed."

If you're still trying to get something from your mother (love, respect, validation, connection . . .) and need to avoid upsetting her, your anger will feel too dangerous. If you have to maintain a certain self-image that excludes anger, you'll also need to keep this emotion at bay. But if you want to champion your wounded inner child, if you want to create room to feel what was too threatening to feel earlier, if you want to release the feeling (rather than stay unconsciously stuck in it), you need to give yourself permission to feel angry.

There is a kind of victim anger that feels whiny and impotent and an empowered anger that feels like standing up for yourself. What I'm talking about is getting to the empowered anger, even though you might start out with the other. Some people find anger easy to do and use it as their all-purpose emotion to stand in for disappointment, sadness, fear—all kinds of things. Others hold their anger in for all they're worth out of a subconscious fear that letting themselves feel it will mean opening floodgates that can't be shut. Healing emotional wounds of any kind involves becoming emotionally fluent, able to experience and distinguish among a vast array of emotions without being slave to any of them.

The journal is a great place for anger, especially since so many people are uncomfortable with anger, and we may have fewer friends to help us hold this than a softer emotion such as sadness. Anger is hard, and sometimes it is hateful. These are not pretty feelings that you readily display to people, yet the journal holds them without judgment.

Working with anger is so much about permission. Many of us have learned to swallow anger, and it generally takes a long time to unlearn this. If we practice journal writing consistently and honestly, it will help undo this habit of self-censorship.

If anger is one of the emotions that you cannot contain and that you act out in harmful ways, you may need to take special precautions. It's important that you be able to calibrate anger, to have it run along a continuum rather than being something that is either "off" or "on." You need to recognize anger when it first arises and have tools for titrating it, being able to control how much is coming through at any given moment, using distraction, breathing, or time-outs to interrupt unwanted escalation. You might consider an anger management class or working with a therapist if you either feel no control over your anger or don't dare to even touch it.

**Exploring your anger (an exercise)**

In this exercise we'll work with what in journaling is called a sentence stem. The first part of the sentence is provided, and you are to complete it with whatever comes to mind, working quickly so that you don't censor yourself. I encourage you to complete this sentence ten times or more, and for this exercise, target your thoughts on your mother:

I am angry that . . .

After you are finished, read all of your answers and notice how you feel. If you want to do some freestyle writing, this is a good time. I also encourage you to reflect on a further issue:

Beneath the anger, I feel . . .

Complete this sentence stem tens times as well. You might also make a list of the things you haven't forgiven your mother for.

## Leaving the past

Those who would rather not go into these inner recesses often use words like *wallowing* when talking about feelings or our relationship with what is unfinished in our past. They throw out words like this to hook our shame and give the message, "Just get over it!"

And to be sure, it is a question we ask ourselves: How long will this go on? My sense is that *we let go of the past when we're done with it!* When we're complete. It's that simple.

At some point other things become far more interesting and the pull of past emotions just can't compete anymore. We've worked the ground, taken out the big stones, and new things are growing—things that captivate and enrich our lives.

This is not to say we won't flinch if someone touches the center of that wound (though maybe we won't), but we will have completed our active grieving and moved on. Until then, try to counter those thoughts that you should be over the past by reminding yourself that although not everyone may need to do this, it's part of the territory for you. No, you didn't ask for it, and you wouldn't have chosen it. Yet because you have this particular legacy and don't want to pass it on (if you are in a parenting role), because somewhere deep inside you have a connection with that undermothered child and want to make things right, you're doing the work—"fighting the good fight" so to speak. It's not the whole work, this grieving and original pain work, but it is part of it.

It is true that there is some danger of getting stuck there. We can make an identity out of any potent experience, especially one that happens early and leaves deep scars. Working through these mother wounds is not easy, and we may need help. The next chapter focuses on psychotherapy, the most common and, in my mind, best place to get this help.

# 8.

# Psychotherapy: Mother Issues and Mothering Needs

Certainly since the beginning of talk therapy, psychotherapists have been listening to clients agonize about their mothers. We've come a long way since then in the proliferation of therapeutic methods, but Mother still figures prominently in therapists' offices.

Today the needs of clients who are undermothered can be addressed in a number of ways.

There is a spectrum of options including the following:

- deep healing work targeted toward birth trauma and pre-birth experiences

- a variety of talk therapies or even expressive therapies (e.g., art, movement therapies) and somatic (body-centered) therapies that help you explore unresolved issues in your relationship with your mother and/or work with unmet developmental needs

- family therapy undertaken with your mother now to improve the relationship

- counseling that helps you develop a more secure attachment in your actual relationships with others (including couples work)

- innovative approaches focused on inner work that help build a positive experience of attachment to any viable attachment figure, including an inner mother, an ideal mother, a spiritual figure, your cat ... (examples include brainspotting, therapies that work with internal "parts," and experiential imagery)

- therapies where the therapist herself (or himself) deliberately serves as an attachment figure and attempts to meet some of these earlier needs (see Re-mothering, p. 135)

These options are not exclusive, so, for example, you might be working with a therapist building your own inner mother at the same time you experience the therapist as a Good Mother figure. And please remember that although more airtime is given to our earliest attachment injuries in this chapter, the issues we deal with in therapy and our unmet developmental needs go far beyond the first few years of life.

Among the hundreds of kinds of psychotherapy, there are strong disagreements about issues like touching clients and how far the therapist should go in meeting needs directly. Most of my discussion will stay within the mainstream, although I will also give examples of work that fall outside of it.

Generally, brief therapies and cognitive-behavioral thera-pies cannot be expected to provide much to those dealing with early childhood wounds. Stated one way, such therapies may affect the neocortex, the thinking brain, but never reach the emotional brain. In most cases, the emotional brain will need to unload its traumas and release its defenses, and this hap-pens most easily in a safe, nurturing relationship that devel-ops over time. Also, according to psychiatrists Thomas Lewis, Fari Amini, and Richard Lannon, authors of *A General Theory of Love*, what allows the emotional brain (limbic brain) of a client to change is falling into limbic resonance with the therapist and being tuned by the therapist's emotional brain, just as the baby's brain was originally tuned by the mother's. This generally takes a number of years; there is no quick fix for reprogramming the emotional brain.

A few other terms may be helpful here. The term *psychodynamic* is often used when speaking of therapies that deeply explore the childhood roots of behavior; when such therapies focus on the reparative effects of the relationship with the therapist, the terms *relational therapy* and *attachment-based psychotherapy* are sometimes used. These are all very different than *attachment therapy,* a controversial therapy used primarily with adopted children who have not attached to their new caregivers.

The discussion that follows relates to long-term depth therapies attuned to early attachment.

### Parallels with the Good Mother

Therapy parallels the mother–child relationship in that it exists to meet the client's needs, not the therapist's, just as the mother is there to meet the child's needs and not vice versa. Like the Good Mother, the therapist attends to you in an attuned way, giving you the space to express anything and everything, being interested in your inner experience, helping you negotiate what is difficult. Some researcher-clinicians even suggest that just as the mother functions as part of the baby's nervous system (albeit an external part) and is a platform for the child's growth, the therapist plays a similar role with a client, offering a taste of new states of consciousness and new ways of relating by entering into shared states in the course of therapy.[66] (Remember limbic resonance.)

The psychiatrist and pediatrician D. W. Winnicott talked about the therapist providing a holding environment, just as the mother provides for the infant. He believed the therapist needs the same patience, tolerance, and reliability as a mother devoted to her infant; must treat the client's wishes as needs; and has to put aside other interests in order to be available.[67] Just as the Good Mother must at first be very accommodating to the baby's needs but over time allows natural frustrations to arise (although in a calibrated fashion), the therapist can back off a little as the client becomes more independent.

Another parallel between therapist and Good Mother is that the relationally attuned therapist keeps a two-prong awareness, always paying attention to what is happening between them at the same time that he or she is helping the client deal with any given problem. While attunement to the feelings of the client is standard in all therapies, not all therapies keep an eye on the relationship dance, especially as it relates to attachment issues. The problem-solving focus of most behavioral, cognitive, and brief forms of therapy generally isn't paying attention to this more subterranean aspect.

For clients who had the types of mothers described in this book, a therapist not paying attention to attachment-related issues is akin to a mother who is somewhat clueless about the child's relational needs. The emotionally absent mother has room in her awareness only for the immediate task at hand, and those who are highly stressed may barely be doing that. She may be responsive to outer needs (to some degree) but not to inner feelings and needs. The emotionally present therapist must be attuned to both.

Unlike the mother who is relationally "blind," the relationally attuned therapist knows that she or he is an important source of constancy for the client. This is something that was missing for those who have been undermothered. They haven't had someone there in that consistent way that you can count on and which is the basis for a sense of security. Therapists who are willing can become this source of constancy and help fill the hole of what was missing in the early environment and missing in the client's psyche.

Often an undermothered adult child will have a great need to feel that the therapist is not just providing care because it's his or her job (like Mom) but that this time the caring is personal. Many adults who were undermothered don't have a sense that their mothers really knew them and consequently didn't have a sense of their mothers liking them. They may have felt their mothers somewhat dutifully loved them (on a superficial level), but people can't feel truly loved (or even liked) if they don't feel seen for who they are. For such a client to feel genuinely liked by the therapist, she must know that her potential as well as her pain is seen.

All of this requires great skill on the part of the therapist. The therapist must show that she genuinely cares yet must keep certain boundaries in order for the relationship to stay clear, professional, and not become enmeshed in the therapist's needs.

### Special considerations in attachment-oriented work

In attachment-oriented therapy, the therapist serves as a new attachment figure, allowing an opportunity to form an attachment bond and work through some of the unresolved issues from earlier relationships. This is a very deep form of work, requiring a number of special skills on the part of therapists.

First, it must be understood that clients with attachment injuries will often be unaware of much of what is affecting them. Because so much of our infant experience is preverbal, it doesn't get encoded and stored as explicit memories do and isn't something we can talk about or are even consciously aware of. These unconscious patterns will likely be lived out by the client both in therapy and in life.

A skilled therapist watches for replays of patterns and reactions, reads the body language of a client, and pays careful attention to his own experience as information about what is going on for the client and what is happening between them. As psychotherapist and author David Wallin writes in *Attachment in Psychotherapy*, "That which we cannot verbalize, we tend to enact with others, to evoke in others, and/or to embody."[68] The quality of our attachment relationships is largely determined by the nonverbal interactions that make them up, he explains.[69] Eye contact, facial expressions, and moving toward or away from are all part of an exquisite dance between infant and mother, between lovers, and between therapist and client.

Because of the regression that will happen at times (the client going back to very early states), there may be feelings of merging in the relationship; these can blur the normal boundaries. Therapists need to be impeccable in not further-ing dependency beyond what is healing and to not use touch or any aspect of their relationship to meet their own needs for affection, power, contact, and so forth. As you can imagine, a codependent therapist who needs to be needed could become entrapping and wounding rather than healing.

In most intensive forms of therapy there will be some ideal-ization of the therapist, who, for a time, will be seen through rose-colored glasses. The therapist is being seen through the eyes of the client's love and need for love. Because we so need this love to fill in for what we missed as a child, we fill in for what may be missing in our therapists, attributing to them more than they actually possess. We see them not as they are but as we need them to be.

This idealization is, for a time, advantageous in that it helps us attach to the therapist, just as a child's idealization of parents is believed to help them attach to parents. While some would posit that all children, out of necessity, idealize their parents, I'm not so sure of this. One woman shared with me that her first remembered experience of her mother was of someone with very limited capacity. At three years old, she felt smarter than her mother. Naturally a three-year-old is not going to have more life knowledge than her mother, but something about this experience is eerily prophetic. The woman grew up to become a doctor, while the mother was a woman of very limited maturity.

Although all forms of therapy involve some vulnerability on the part of clients, dealing with our earliest abandonment wounds and allowing feelings of neediness and dependency to arise in the therapeutic relationship really accentuates this feeling of vulnerability. It takes tremendous trust on the part of the client to tolerate and express these feelings, and therapists must know how to deal with this respectfully and skillfully.

As you can see, working with early attachment issues is very delicate business, and clearly not every therapist or form of therapy is suited to it. In the attachment-oriented work I am describing, the relationship becomes the vehicle for healing. In other therapies, the relationship has to be sturdy enough to hold the other elements, but the various interventions are believed to be the more specific vehicle for healing.

### Touch in therapy

Most therapists are trained to restrict or avoid touching their clients. In psychodynamic therapy, the need for touch is explored, but it is considered "acting out" to bring those touch needs into the relationship rather than help the client "work through" them. Therapists who are more "body-centered" or whose training has been less traditional often feel differently about it. Some will employ touch to help calm a client who is extremely agitated; others may use touch as part of helping clients tune in to their experience, and yet others may feel that offering an occasional touch is important for clients who, because of their history, have so often felt untouchable. One trauma expert remarked that there may come a time when *not* touching your client becomes unethical, because it is withholding such an essential element of healing.

When dealing with early attachment injuries, the issues related to touch are heightened more than usual. Often clients may come with higher-than-average touch deprivation and touch hunger. They feel a greater need for touch, and touch has greater impact with them.

One therapist allowed her client to express her needs for contact and support by allowing the client to take hold of her hand or make contact with the therapist's foot by reaching out with her own foot. The primal need for contact was met, and the client's fears about rejection and constraints about reaching out were easily accessed without the kind of body contact that could have been confusing.

Adults who have had touch sexualized inappropriately as children or who are overstimulated by touch or tactilely defensive will have specific vulnerabilities. Touch may feel too powerful to them or too threatening. It's a very complex issue.

Most therapists whose training includes touch have learned to always ask permission before touching and to verbalize what they are going to do. ("Is it okay if I touch your shoulder as we do this? I'm just going to touch you right here, like this. How does that feel?")

A therapist might accept a client initiating touch when it reflects an important step for the client, as for example, the client above who would reach for her therapist's hand when working through issues from her early life where it felt too dangerous to reach out or to have needs. If a client's touch feels seductive, manipulative, or as if the client is not respecting boundaries, the therapist will need to confront this.

### Re-mothering

Occasionally one will find a therapist who is willing to more directly take on the role of "surrogate mother" and also more willing to touch. One such therapist offers "re-mothering therapy" to adult women. She encourages her clients to relax into their dependency and attachment needs and let them be met. "Instead of shaming undermothered women for being hungry for love, I take their hunger for love seriously," therapist Soonja Kim writes.[70] She is there, as the Good Mother, willing (most radically) to love them. This includes holding clients who want to be held and affirming them with what I have called Good Mother messages.

Soonja Kim invites her clients to settle back and take in this loving attention:

> *Passive love is the kind of love where care is offered, without your having to do much to elicit it. It requires more intuitiveness and empathy on the part of the giver, and more receptivity of the taker. Receiving passive love can be deeply healing for undermothered women, who had to be so active in trying to earn love. They have so much shame around their emotional neediness, that to be given, without having to disclose their needs directly, feels extremely comforting.[71]*

Kim goes on to say:

> *As you feel your dependency and attachment needs sweetly embraced by a mothering figure, and allow yourself to receive passive love, there proceeds a gradual relaxation in your body, heart, mind, and spirit. In that relaxation, you may first go through the grieving period of not having the care and the sweet love you needed growing up. However, as you allow the grieving to flow and to be released, you can move to a deeper level of relaxation, where you can access who you really are. You also may experience the truth of your interconnectedness with all beings that releases you from the deep sense of aloneness you have felt.[72]*

Many would agree that relaxing into a deeper connection and one's underlying essential nature is a much-needed healing. Some would say it is our birthright, lost when mothers can't support a baby's presence.

Work of this nature sometimes requires something outside the traditional fifty-minute hour. It may require sessions that are several hours and that may on occasion take special forms. One woman, nearly fifty, recounted a series of sessions she had with her therapist after working by phone on issues related to her emotionally absent mother for over a year. She traveled to her therapist's town and stayed in a nearby motel so she could do several long sessions, even including some nonsession time with the therapist's family. (Keep in mind that we are talking about loving human contact and inclusion for a person who never felt wanted by her mother.)

Here is the woman's description of breaking through to her deepest core of infant pain and what it meant to be held by her therapist.

> *I was weeping from my core and the depth of my being, and at that moment more than anything, I needed the embrace of love to hold me, contain me, which my therapist did. After a while, it was as if it wasn't just my therapist holding me, though I know she was there.*

> [Later] *I would feel an amazing sense that I had been held by Love itself, that it went beyond my therapist and her family, and was something so much deeper. We had touched a core reality, and that embrace of love, for me, is a metaphor of the love and embrace I needed my whole life. The longing to be wanted, really wanted; to be acknowledged that I even exist and don't have to earn the right to exist and be alive; that I am beautiful and lovable (to be held and not treated like poison)—well, what more can be said?*

This early re-mothering is powerful medicine that is not always handled well. I've heard of a number of therapists who provide holding, sustained eye contact, healing verbal messages, and sometimes even a baby bottle. Clients have reported mixed results, and I've heard of some serious injury when the therapist abandoned a client who had previously been encouraged to regress into a dependent state. Other times the work has been benign but not always on target for the client. The first rule of good mothering is attunement, so even well-intentioned and compassionate therapists who are not quite in synch with a client aren't going to have the best results.

I believe it is authentic, attuned, trustworthy, and respectful connection that heals, and that is not something a therapist can pull out of his pocket like certain other kinds of interventions. I thus place more trust in needs and responses that organically arise in therapy rather than are applied in a formulaic way.

This was how it was in my own experience of being re-mothered by a therapist. The felt need for re-mothering arose from deep within me after working on other early trauma for several years. As others have reported, it felt like a hole in my heart where Mother was supposed to be. When I indicated to my therapist that I wanted her to stand in for my mother, she was momentarily reluctant. (It goes against so much of our professional training.) But then she responded in the way her heart dictated and really showed up for me. She did not offer to hold me (and I never asked), but she wasn't afraid of touch, which was really healing for me. I think our deepest bonding happened through gazing deeply into each other's eyes. The connection went through the eyes and straight into my heart. It was a profound experience for me, and this bonding (which I reinforced internally) resulted, over time, in reorganizing my entire experience of myself and of life. It provided me the chance to experience the essential ingredients I had missed, which allowed my development to move ahead by leaps and bounds. Speaking about it later, I said the most important element in that therapy had been the fact that in a very tangible and real way I felt loved.

## From isolation to secure attachment

When things go well in therapy, we grow and develop new options. People who have sworn off vulnerability may learn to tolerate vulnerability enough to actually let someone in. Here is an example of the progression that a person with a self-sufficient strategy might go through with a therapist:

### 1. Protective isolation

The self-protective stance is not letting others in. This is a defense against the pain of possible rejection. The self-sufficient person has concluded that love isn't going to be there, so it's better not to want it. Any expression of warmth and affection unsettles this stance.

### 2. Cracks in the armor

The therapist who is patient and attuned will eventually find ways to help the client feel seen and understood, melting some of the protective armor.

### 3. Ambivalence and longing

As more contact is tolerated, repressed longings come to the surface and fight with the old defenses. Now there is both a "stop" and "go" message, with attending ambivalence.

### 4. Melting

Because the longing has been so repressed, it is very strong when it breaks through. Indeed, it's strong enough to melt the resistance, leaving the client feeling exposed and vulnerable.

### 5. Fear

Feeling vulnerable and dependent may set off tremendous alarm bells. This is something the self-sufficient have learned to avoid at all costs.

### 6. Insecurity

If the fear can be navigated, more attachment continues to form, and the therapist becomes very important to the client. This is often hard for the client to tolerate. Therapists go away (on vacation or for work) and are available on a limited basis. The adult part of the client understands this, but the attachment needs of the infant that are aroused go far beyond an hour a week. Absorbed into the feelings of the infant self, the client may feel as if she needs the therapist for her very survival. When the therapist goes away, the client caught in these states may fear that the therapist will not return or perhaps won't care about her in the same way.

### 7. Drinking in the nurturance

Even with feelings of insecurity, the client increasingly is able to take in and enjoy the nurturance that is offered, feeling gratitude and satisfaction.

### 8. Increasing security of the bond

As the bond between therapist and client continues to strengthen, it becomes sturdier and more resilient. Disruptions to the relationship (a vacation, a misunderstanding) are more easily tolerated, and the client needs less reassurance.

### 9. Healthy entitlement

In time and with consistently positive response, the client begins to feel more confident and deserving and to ask for what she wants. This has a positive effect on self-confidence and on other relationships.

## 10. Internalizing the attachment figure

Both the attachment figure's presence and the good feelings that constitute the relationship become part of the client's psyche and structure. In a secure attachment, that person becomes part of your heart. (See "Your portable Good Mother," p. 157)

Although I am describing a self-sufficient style that begins with protective isolation, it's an isolation that isn't always obvious. Attachment wounds can stay hidden for a long time. The client going through these stages may have comfortable and close friendships that do not stir up and do not have the same power to heal the attachment wounds that lie under the surface. An adult with a self-sufficient style may even have a stable marriage that lasts for decades but is just distant enough not to rock the attachment boat. Although I have described this process in the context of a close therapeutic relationship, a similar process could happen with any potential attachment figure who stays consistently present and supports this evolution.

### Therapist as "Teaching Mommy"

One of the most difficult things for clients in an intensely relational process like this is to understand that even though the therapist is providing a yummy, long-desired experience of the Good Mommy, one that the client might wish to bask in forever, the therapist is there as a temporary stand-in. The therapist is standing in while you develop your own Good Mother inside. The therapist in all her tenderness, wisdom, and patience is simply showing you how it is done, when it is done well. She is what I call the Teaching Mommy, meaning that she is there to model this, to show your adult self how to do it.

It is the inner mother that will be there on Christmas Day or a long weekend or the middle of the night, not the therapist. Of course to the extent you have internalized the therapist, you can pull her up anytime.

Even without referring directly to an inner mother, we could say the therapist jump-starts aspects of yourself that haven't been working, like being able to provide support or appropriately protect yourself. We don't want these to be available only in the therapist's office. A skilled therapist will help the client incorporate these capacities so that they are available 24/7.

# 9.

# Connecting with Good Mother Energy

In order to heal, we need to not only acknowledge and grieve what was missing but also find ways to make up for it. In making up for a nurturing deficit and a mother who was not fully present, we need to connect with "Good Mother energy." Fortunately, there are many ways we can do this (besides therapy), and this chapter will focus on three of them: connecting with the Good Mother archetype, finding others who stand in for the Good Mother, and working through unresolved issues and unmet needs in primary relationships.

## Opening to the Good Mother

If you repressed your needs and longing for a good mother, as so many of us have, it can feel pretty intense when this thaws out and the lost feelings emerge. The longing may feel unfamiliar, dangerous, embarrassing, but it is vital to the healing process. The desire for mothering is natural; it was there when you were a child, even if you learned to turn it off as a strategy for survival. As one therapist reminds her clients, the yearning itself is healthy. It is part of being human to want to be nurtured and cared for.

Although this longing may have been totally frustrated in the past, it can bear fruits now. We can receive the nurture, care, guidance, protection, mirroring, and so on from others whom we now *choose* to put in these roles. Eventually we can develop a strong Good Mother within us, modeled on the best of what we've experienced or perhaps on our experiences with the archetypal Good Mother.

Regardless of which of these levels you're working on, the dynamic is really the same. The Good Mother can't give to you if you're stuck in a funk about how unmothered you feel. She can't tenderly stroke your face when you defiantly turn away. You must allow yourself to be vulnerable and let her draw near. Only then will you receive her gifts.

## Archetypes

Archetypes are larger-than-life patterns that we, as humans, imperfectly embody. They are larger than life because they are broader than any one expression of them. For example, there is not just one way a person embodying the crone will appear; one wise elder may be more extroverted or idiosyncratic than another. Archetypes are like the basic roles filled by new actors in every play. Every culture, like every theater director, casts them a little differently, but we see the same basic character types again and again.

This is not simply a matter of convention, according to those who experience archetypes in the realm of subtle energies. The same archetypes show up again and again because they exist as "energy fields" in the larger transpersonal realm. Many of these archetypes have been recognized since the beginning of human culture, although in earlier times these basic energies were associated more with the natural world. Long before Mother Mary embodied the mother archetype, there was Mother Earth. Goddess cultures related to the earth as the source of nurture and supply and primary mother image. They each had their own name and own image of this archetype, but they all knew her.

When the Swiss psychiatrist Carl Jung brought archetypes into modern psychology early in the twentieth century, he described them as residues of ancestral memory preserved in the collective unconscious (greater mind) that we all share. From a Jungian view, we are born with an archetype of the Good Mother as a psychic structure. This archetype is like a blueprint that gets turned on or becomes operative when we meet mothering that is "good enough."[73]

When this doesn't happen in our families of origin, we might find someone else to activate this archetype, such as a therapist, as described in the previous chapter. The therapist becomes the embodiment and the doorway to the deeper energies of the archetype, which may later be experienced in additional ways, as described below.

## Working with imagery and symbols

We often experience the archetypes through powerful imagery. This may happen in dreams, guided imagery, and artwork. Some of the archetypal forces that may appear include the Good Mother, particular aspects of the mother such as those enumerated in chapter 2, the bad mother/witch, the abandoned child, and the starving, primitive instinctual self.

Carla, a woman in her forties, reported that she often met a protective mother bear figure in all of these venues (meditations, dreams, and art creations). She found herself creating mother–infant pairs and drawing circles, which many would associate with a mother's breast and which she associated with the mother, the womb, and being contained in a safe space. For Carla, these expressed the longing for maternal aspects that had been missing in her life. She had not been protected and received little nurturing and almost no time alone with her mother.

Carla experienced her cutoff instinctual desire as a primitive creature-child so voracious that it could eat her alive.

Remember that whatever is pushed into the unconscious gathers force. We can't cut off our instinctual needs and float above them without having some kind of counterbalance periodically erupt out of our personal underworld.

Making a representation of the Good Mother is a good way to bring that archetype deeper into your consciousness, and I encourage you to take the time to do this. It can be a collage, a drawing, a sculpture—any number of things. The idea is to anchor the ideal mother and give her a form. You can then use that form to evoke her energy when doing inner work.

You might also make a list of Good Mother messages and of qualities associated with this archetype. I actually wrote my Good Mother messages on the collage I made.

## Help from the Divine Mother

One of the classic images associated with the mother archetype is Mother Mary from the Christian tradition. The Madonna and Child is one of the most frequently painted images in existence. It is an image found well before the Christian era and seems to have universal appeal. *Mary* is one of many names beginning with the syllable *Ma,* meaning "mother." Mother Mary is often associated with the rose, which is linked with the same Great Mother energy.

Many people have reported receiving comfort and guidance from Mary or from mother figures of other religious traditions, such as Kuan Yin (or Guan Yin), the bodhisattva of compassion. Most, if not all, traditions have images of the Divine Mother, and believers within these traditions often have experiences in which they feel loved and cared for by this maternal energy.

One woman described feeling like a cranky baby who was able to let go and relax when she felt held by a loving presence that felt to her like Mother Mary. Another experienced something akin to this when she imagined being wrapped in swaddling clothes by the Goddess Mother. A third woman, Ann, described doing some inner journey work and meeting a goddess figure who seemed to take away her burdens and absorb her pain. Ann discovered that she could call on this being in times of need. I would categorize all of these experiences as the equivalent of Mother as Modulator experienced internally.

Sometimes the answer is to be mothered, and sometimes it is to become the mother. This is true on the human level, but it can also happen on the spiritual level. Ariel, who was very undermothered, turned to the goddess tradition to provide a positive model of the mother and the deep feminine, finding it healing and transformative. She considers herself a priestess now, which is not a designation assigned by any religious authority but simply means being a channel for the divine feminine energy. Her job is to embody this energy. Good Mother energy is the energy of nourishment and love, Ariel told me. The Great Mother is the matrix, the web of interconnectivity that holds us all.

Devotional practices to any of the Divine Mother figures help open the heart to the Good Mother archetype and can eventually help replace the image of a withholding mother with something more generous and warm. We need models for developing the Good Mother within, and those coming from spiritual traditions are potent for many.

### Taking on the "good" of the Good Mother

Whether feeling a child of the Cosmic Mother or bonding with a person (of either gender) who assumes the role of Good Mother, there are definite benefits to a secure relationship.

Connecting with the Good Mother allows us to appropriate some of her qualities, whether her confidence, her graciousness, her generosity, or other desirable qualities. Just as securely attached children feel that the physical dwelling they live in with their family is very much theirs as well (a feeling not always shared by those with an orphan complex), those fully and securely attached to Mommy are free to partake of her nature and make themselves at home there. This may take the form of imitating external behaviors of Mother, the way she stands or tilts her head, but it can also occur on a deeper level where the child feels that she is part of Mommy's heart and that Mother's qualities feel like part of her, too.

The child who adores his mother also takes on some of the halo around this idealization. The securely attached child who feels "My mommy is really special" may also feel "and I'm special because I'm part of her." This is related to Mother as Source (p. 21).

## A second chance at finding a Good Mother

Fortunately, we have a second chance as an adult to receive the mothering we missed earlier in our lives. We might even experience this in more than one relationship. We might find ourselves receiving love, nurturance, guidance, encouragement, mirroring, protection, and the other Good Mother functions in multiple places: from our partners, therapists, close friends, in-laws, spiritual teachers, mentors, and from the mother that we eventually develop within ourselves.

To have someone consistently there for us is a great blessing, if we can take it in. If we cling to an earlier lack of love and don't take it in, then it can't heal us. It may take sitting through discomfort, struggling through feelings of unworthiness and learning to trust, but receiving this nurturance is essential to healing mother wounds.

When we see that what is offered is given *out of love* rather than out of obligation, we feel deeply touched. (Children of emotionally absent mothers often feel that any caring from their mothers came out of obligation.) If we can take in this freely given love and care, eventually we will develop a healthy sense of entitlement, the sense that our needs matter and we have a right to be supported and nurtured. Slowly our stance will change to a sense of positive expectancy that our needs will be met.

For this to happen, our Good Mother substitutes need to be generous with us: generous with their attention, their affection, generous with praise, and generous in giving us the space we need to work things out. Since emotionally absent, nonexpressive, and neglectful mothers don't give much, this generosity is a key ingredient in healing. We are often surprised to learn that the generous mother finds pleasure in meeting our needs. This pleasure forms part of her development, too.

Obviously the people in these Good Mother roles must feel safe to you. What is happening is nothing less than a radical transformation, changing your self-image, how you are in relationships, and awakening the child states that have been frozen inside. If you developed a hardened defense structure and have taken on the critical voices of those around you, healing will require stepping out of this. You need to be soft and receptive, like a trusting child asleep in Mother's arms, so you must find people who elicit this in you and who are trustworthy.

Remember that it is a journey, a long journey. Children don't grow up overnight. And while the goal is to heal the wounded parts of your psyche and become a healthy and whole adult, this happens in stages. I find it most helpful to think of this in terms of the inner child being healed, but you can think of it as simply filling in deficits or strengthening your system so you can absorb those nutrients that were lacking earlier.

## Meeting mothering needs with partners

Naturally, a place we look for our unmet needs to be fulfilled is in our relationships with romantic partners. This is both an excellent choice and a troublesome one. Love relationships can be a place we feel cared for, tenderly held, treasured. They're great for snuggling, for meeting touch needs, and for our undefended, sweet selves to show up. But they are also so much more. Often they are partnerships in terms of household and material life, and frequently include raising children. Relationships with partners are the primary place where our sexual needs are met. They are also where we have responsibility for nurturing and caring for another. The existence of so many simultaneous roles creates some special requirements for meeting unmet childhood needs here.

Here are some questions that may help you look at your current relationship if you are in one. If you are not with a partner, you could use the same questions to reflect on a past relationship:

> What psychological and material needs does your relationship fulfill? Does either of you take on Good Mother roles with the other? Which ones?

> Does one of you do more nurturing than the other, or do you take turns? Is there a parent–child component to the relationship?

It can cause trouble when we're trying to get earlier needs met yet have no conscious agreements about this. When we begin the dating or mating dance, we're usually not asking, "Will you be my mother?" Partners can feel resentful to find themselves enlisted in this role without their consent. Especially if they get no time off.

It works better when we give our partners choices and negotiate for specific needs to be met. We can ask for these in adult ways: "Can you hold me a while? I am feeling lonely and insecure." "The child inside me feels scared right now and wants to hear you say it's going to be all right." "I need you to mirror back my feelings right now, so I know that I'm heard." It's best when the "adult you" can do the negotiation. There are many good books and classes that can help you learn to ask for what you want. (If talking about the inner child or "child parts" feels totally foreign to you, you may want to skip ahead to the next chapter and then come back.)

This doesn't mean the child parts of you can't also have a relationship with your partner. It might be helpful for the adult you to be protective enough of this child to assess what's reasonable within a particular relationship and to take the lead in negotiating that. Child parts can step forward and make requests, too, but it is best if they understand that the partner isn't the only adult around. You might decide that the bulk of your inner child work and re-parenting can better be done elsewhere, but that it's nice to also have your partner nurture your child on occasion.

In romantic relationships, we also need to be willing to exchange roles and to provide nurture, protection, and care to our partners. This can be done as an adult-to-adult exchange or a nurturing parent-to-child exchange where one partner is acting as a nurturing parent to the child in the other. There can also be exchanges between child states in each of the adult partners. When you're both wounded children, there can be much hurt and blame, but two children learning about resilience and trust can have some fun together.

It's important to remember that our adult partners don't owe us the selfless love that we wanted from our mothers. They have needs and limitations, and we are adults now, responsible for ourselves. That doesn't mean you can't have vulnerable feelings, even some needs that are rooted in infancy, but it does mean that your partner has a choice about responding to these needs, which ultimately are your responsibility. Having your partner meet these needs is only one of many options. If your partner fails to do so at any particular moment, there are other options. It's important that you not get so absorbed in your child feelings that you forget this.

An example of an infancy pattern that might get played out between partners is trying to remain within the oneness of the early merged state in which babies feel themselves as part of Mother. This is referred to as a "fused" relationship. When two people are fused, they don't know themselves as separate, distinct individuals. Part of what makes falling in love so intoxicating for many people is reexperiencing this sense of oneness. In time, enough differences naturally arise that the sense of oneness disappears and each partner feels him- or herself as separate. If you haven't had enough merging, you might resist this and try to hold on to the sense of oneness. This will cause trouble, because if you can't see your partner as separate from you, you can't really be attentive to your partner's needs.

When early needs are prominent in a relationship, we can become hostage to these needs. Some people find it difficult to leave relationships because they've projected onto the partner many basic parenting needs and are developmentally unprepared to walk away from Mother.

## Repeating the past

Many therapists believe that adults unconsciously repeat unhealthy patterns from their early parent–child relationships— for example, picking partners who are unavailable in ways that are similar to how a parent was unavailable. In these cases healing is often a matter of becoming aware of the pattern, working through these childhood wounds in therapy or other places, and making new choices in terms of love relationships. Trying to extract from a partner who is like Mommy what you didn't get from Mommy is usually not successful.

It is, however, common. There are entire therapies that revolve around the idea that we are attracted to people who have the same deficits as our parents in an unconscious attempt to heal the original injury. In approaches like Imago Relationship Therapy, therapists help partners use the difficulties in the relationship to bring up earlier injuries and heal them. Emotionally Focused Couples Therapy is another approach that uses the couple relationship to repair attachment injuries. From this view it's not that partners made the wrong choice—they made the perfect choice for healing.

The following self-queries may help you examine your own patterns.

> Write a paragraph describing how you experienced your mother as a young child. It doesn't need to be full sentences; you could even make a list of adjectives. Then write a paragraph about how you experienced any significant romantic partners and look for similarities. (Note that significant partners are not necessarily long-lasting relationships but are very often emotionally charged ones.)

> What are the sources of conflict and upset in your relationship? Do these mirror any elements from early childhood?

> What indications of earlier unfinished business or of insecure attachment can you see in your current relationship?

> At this point in your life, can you be with someone whose heart is steady, patient, welcoming, with plenty of love, or do you tend to find people who are skittish and not fully there?

Some examples of unmet childhood needs that show up in adult life include the following:

• needing an inordinate amount of support and reassurance

• feeling insecure, jealous, and angry when your partner is not responsive to your needs right away

• being unable to tolerate your partner's absence

• maintaining a fused relationship, "joined at the hip," as

we often say

- projecting onto your partner negative qualities of your mother

- elevating your partner to a one-up position and feeling that he or she is smarter, is more capable, or somehow has more value than you

- tolerating an unusual amount of abandonment or unavailability of your partner or reacting to it in ways reminiscent of how you felt as a child

- not expecting emotional closeness from your partner (because you didn't get it from your mother and don't expect it from anyone)

### The healing power of secure romantic attachments

Author Susan Anderson says in *The Journey from Abandonment to Healing* that in a secure relationship, a romantic partner serves a similar function as a mother does for a securely attached child. In both cases, the relationship provides a primary sense of belonging, security, and connectedness. Speaking of adults, she writes, "Many people function as well as they do precisely because they feel so secure in their primary relationships. They are self-confident, self-directed, and content because they know someone is there for them." Ruptures in such a relationship can seriously undermine this confidence and well-being.[74]

Indeed, partner relationships have often been found to be good for people, leading to benefits like better health and longer life spans. They can also be the cauldron in which insecurely attached adults finally become securely attached and reap its many benefits.

### A chance to be held (an exercise)

Here is an exercise you can do with a partner or a friend. It is a chance to be held by a safe person and let yourself receive without in that moment needing to earn it or give anything back. It is perhaps most healing if you imagine your inner child receiving this. Think of how often we hear women complain they want to be cuddled, but that's hard to get without their partner turning it into a sexual opportunity. Well here is one chance to get some of those early needs met.

Find a partner for this exercise who can agree to the guidelines and intention of providing safe, nonsexual holding.

This is a reciprocal exercise in which each gets a chance to be held and to be the one who provides the holding, so decide which role you want to take first. It's helpful to agree on a set period of time for each partner to receive; twenty minutes is a good guideline.

The basic instruction is that the person who provides the holding does not stroke or comfort the other, but is there more as a simple, accepting presence. Often this exercise is done having both parties sit on the floor, with the "child" in front and the "good parent" leaning back against the wall for support. Pillows may be used to provide a soft backdrop and also to somewhat buffer the body contact. The child leans back against, perhaps resting on, the chest of the person in the good-parent role, and the "good parent" wraps her arms around the "child." The person being held can change position as

desired. When in the receiving role, do your best to relax into and really take in this very primal form of support and nurture. Do not talk during this period.

After you've switched roles, allow a time to verbally
discuss what the experience was like for you.

Acknowledge yourself for having the courage and commitment to try something experimental. If it went well
and was satisfying for both, you can set a time to do it
again!

One woman reported that during her first experience of
this exercise, she kept anxiously checking every few minutes,
preparing herself for her partner's abandonment. After about
ten minutes of her partner's steady presence, she was able to
let go and really take in that she was being held and that the
container was safe enough that she could rest in it. It was a
profound experience and a new feeling that she was "worth
staying for." Think how many young children have not had
this quality time and the sense of being important enough for
Mother to give all of her attention to for more than the brief-
est moment. Exercises such as this can help change this deep
imprint.

## Your portable Good Mother

Just as it is believed that a young child constructs a picture of his mother that he carries around inside and that helps in the process of eventually separating and differentiating from Mother, so building an internal sense of a Good Mother figure creates, in essence, a portable Good Mother that you carry around with you.

This might simply be a conglomeration of memories of the person, but it can be more than that, too. It can be an internalization of the person's love and support. One time I had an image of my therapist holding my heart between her hands and supporting me with great tenderness and devotion. It felt like I could take this image into my heart where it became a layer of me. I also dialogue with my therapist in my journal frequently, where sometimes she says surprising things, though never out of keeping with the person I know her to be.

The process of taking in and internalizing Good Mother energy is not a purely mental or psychological process. To steep in any of these good feelings requires letting them saturate the body. Here is a short practice you can use to aid the process of internalizing any feeling or resource state you want to strengthen. You could use it to take in the nurturing of a person in your life, helping you connect with the Good Mother archetype or even one of the Good Mother roles described in chapter 2.

**Strengthening a resource state (an exercise)**

Start with consciously choosing what it is that you want to feel more deeply and incorporate into yourself. As you begin with the simple intention of tuning in to this, notice how you first register your awareness of it. Does it come as a visual image, a particular feeling in your body, through another sensory channel or combination of channels?

Notice how it affects your breathing and your muscle tone. Does it bring warmth or coolness to your body? Any other sensation?

Can you bring this feeling all the way through your body and into your toes?

How does feeling this affect your posture? Does it open up or support specific places?

Notice any memories or images that come to mind.

What can you use to remind yourself of this experience? (This could be an image, a word, a memory of a feeling in your body.)

Naturally, the more often you use a practice like this, the more vivid and enduring the result will be.

When you internalize an attachment figure, or any wisdom figure, you can turn to this figure in times of need. Having this as part of you gives you more resilience. In the next chapter, we'll expand this to include the Good Mother you cultivate inside yourself.

# 10.

# Inner Child Work

You may have heard the phrase *The child is father to the man*,[75] which means the child is the foundation upon which adult life is built. What kind of foundation we have is critical. A resilient child serves as the foundation for a resilient adult.

Unfortunately, some of us never got to that level of resilience in childhood. The child parts carry too many wounds and thus are the foundation of a wounded adult. Even if these wounds are for the most part well managed and out of sight, they leak out at times and we act immaturely.

Fortunately, it's never too late to heal these childhood wounds and for a resilient child to emerge, serving as the foundation for a healthy, resilient adult.

## An introduction to inner child work

All of this talk about wounded inner children creates a lot of discomfort for some, who have little patience for children, inner or otherwise. The notion of an inner child is met with the same irritation as has met all too many actual children.

Yet millions of people have found it helpful to work with the inner child, or what I prefer to call *child states*. I use this term because I find the notion that there is only one inner child is often inaccurate. When used this way, it is often confused with inner life in general, and more specifically feelings and impulses. I think this is an error. Every time you feel sad or angry, that's not necessarily your inner child.

We are very complex beings. Far from having one stable personality, we have many different parts, which come into play at different times. We have child states that hold different beliefs, feelings, and memories, sometimes clustering around a certain age. Some of these child states are wise, some are creative, and some carry specific experiences, such as trauma or the abandonment wound. If we really want to understand ourselves and be as whole as we can be, it will help to know these various inner child states. Because it is at times very awkward to use the plural, I revert at times to referring to the inner child in the singular, but this is only to make it flow better with the text.

The primary methods used in inner child work have been the following:

- using guided meditation, imagery, or hypnotic trance to meet and interact with child states

- pulling out old photographs from childhood to help access memories and feelings from that time

- working with dolls, teddy bears, or similar props to either access child feelings or as part of the adult learning to nurture and protect the inner child

- using art as a medium, especially for young child states to express themselves

- writing letters to an inner child or from an inner child as a way of establishing contact

- dialoguing between adult and child states through journal writing, internal self-talk, or through techniques such as the Voice Dialogue Method

Inner child work is something you can do on your own, in workshops, or with a therapist. It's important enough that even if you are introduced to it by a teacher or therapist and even if you use therapy sessions to go deeper with it, you will want to have ways to also continue these relationships at home. The rest of this chapter will focus on work you can do on your own.

The book that I find offers the most practical and helpful guidance in this is *Recovery of Your Inner Child* by Lucia Capacchione. It has more than forty exercises that cover a range of activities. Capacchione has made great use of art and writing to communicate with inner child states and popularized the practice of switching hands to help distinguish between inner adult and child, turning to the nondominant hand to express the child.

John Bradshaw's bestselling book *Homecoming: Reclaiming and Championing Your Inner Child* makes considerable use of letter writing and the use of affirmations for supplying Good Parent messages that were missing earlier. He works through different developmental stages—a good idea—although I find his descriptions of these stages to be more Freudian than I'm comfortable with. I think you can become responsive to inner kids and their needs without the theoretical filter of things like Oedipal complexes.

Often we are unaware of these inner child states, yet we are blended with them, feeling the same kinds of emotions and needs that we experienced as a child. We may be having a teenage fit or a two-year-old tantrum, feel clingy or insecure, get fixated on self-soothing, or feel young and vulnerable.

If we're willing, we can learn to identify these aspects, differentiating them. This allows us to form conscious relationships with them, which brings in the element of choice.

Some believe that we never outgrow our inner children, and the goal is for them to be happy and healthy. Others see the process of working with inner child states as ideally leading to integration of these parts into the adult.

I don't really have a preference: It's nice either way. It is great to have a sweet and spunky kid inside, and it's great to incorporate their positive qualities into your adult self. Clearly, in working with inner child states, things will change.

Just as children grow up by having their needs met, meeting the previously unmet needs of inner children allows them to mature. Parts of self that revolve around such needs may then fade or dissolve. Other child states come bearing important gifts, qualities that were often cut off and lost in our own childhood which can now be reclaimed. Some of these are the qualities of the natural child described below.

### The child as mother to the self

Just as we have the understanding that the child is father to the man, we could say the child is mother to the real self. As it is usually expressed, the child is the essence of this real self. This is how Carl Jung described the archetype of the child, which he viewed as a symbol of wholeness.

This archetype is also referred to as the natural child or the divine child. Some of the qualities of this child include:

- honesty and genuineness
- sweetness and generosity, a loving heart
- innocence and "beginner's mind"
- openness and trust
- imagination and intuitive knowing
- curiosity
- wonder, awe, and an attitude of play
- spontaneity and the ungroomed, natural behaviors we enjoy in young children
- vitality and aliveness

Most of those who advocate for inner child work do so with the hope not only of healing the wounded child but also of reclaiming these wonderful child qualities.

## "Parts work"

Many inner child states have been identified: the natural child (above), the vulnerable child, the wounded child, the neglected/abandoned child, and the angry child, to name the most common. We also have various "adult" parts—for example, parts that are nurturing and others that are critical.

With an awareness of these many different aspects, it is natural to talk of "parts work." This is a common way that people think of it for themselves, and the language is being adopted by some therapies as well.

### Parts! Yikes! Am I falling apart?

Often all it takes to begin an exploration of these inner parts is simply permission to think in these terms and a willingness to set aside skepticism and fear and start paying attention. By paying attention to your feelings, your behavioral patterns, your inner commentaries, and your body language, you can begin to tune in to various parts of yourself that are shaping your experience.

These parts have their own needs, motivations, beliefs, memories, and particular "style." It's helpful to give them names or, better yet, ask them their names. Is it Crabby Appleton you're facing in the moment, or Sweet Innocence? They will feel very different, their voices will be different (if you give voice to them or hear them in your mind), and how they feel in your body will be different.

Some people find it unsettling to think of seemingly independent parts functioning within them like separate personalities. They think of what we used to call *multiple personality disorder* (now called *dissociative identity disorder* or DID) and get frightened. The difference is that the parts of a person with DID are more completely separated from consciousness and don't so easily relate and coexist. With DID, a person "loses time" and is stunned to find evidence of behaviors she knows nothing about. The switching from one part to another is involuntary, and the parts are generally born of trauma. As people with DID work with these parts, the parts can become more aware of each other and work more cooperatively, which is the aim of most of the parts work therapies that are applicable to all populations.

Some of the newer therapies emphasize that in all of us, these alternate selves are "like real people" with their own style and energetic fingerprint. We seem to be moving toward more understanding and acceptance of the natural multiplicity in all systems, including the human person. If you don't find strange clothes in your closet and people don't come up to you and call you by a different name, your multiplicity doesn't have to interfere with your life.

Who doesn't have a pouting child? An irritated critic? It's okay to have these parts, but it's preferable to get to know them, to "catch ourselves in the act," and to choose where we want to be operating out of.

I find it especially helpful to name the parts and associate them with an image of some kind. You can use art materials and even incorporate photographs of yourself if this feels helpful. You can also use objects of various sorts (such as a stuffed animal). Often you'll start with a particular representation, which, like any image, is a snapshot of a moment in time, and it will change. You may have multiple representations that combine and evolve in all sorts of creative ways. The following is the story of my work with Maria:

## Maria's Story: From Stone Child to Sweet Child

Maria began seriously doing parts work when she recognized the hole left by an emotionally absent mother. She had also experienced physical abuse in the family, and when prompted in therapy to contact an inner child, the only child she could find was a "ghost child" who seemed flimsy and insubstantial. Maria had almost no happy memories from childhood to draw on in finding resilient child parts. She agreed to buy some art materials for future parts work.

Immediately after buying the art supplies, Maria was surprised when she heard an insistent inner voice instructing her to make a representation of it. With red construction paper, glitter, and pictures cut out of wrapping paper, she made an image of a child whose name was Strawberry. Maria recognized Strawberry as the resilient child who was born out of our several years of work together and her secure attachment to me, her therapist. Strawberry was full of spunk, unschooled wisdom, and affection. Many would say Strawberry was the natural child, and Maria saw her as the child she would have been if she had received the nurturing that would have allowed her to blossom. Strawberry became a source of comfort and guidance to Maria and various wounded child parts.

Some of these wounded parts included the Abandoned Baby (with a red, oozing hole in her heart); the Stone Child, which represented a state of shock; and Holy Rage, the anger related to her abuse. Maria also made a representation and dialogued with a part she called Sweet Innocence, which represented her original unharmed nature.

In time, working both at home and in therapy, the Stone Child was dissolved. Holy Rage also receded and disappeared off the stage. Before doing this, Holy Rage asked to be acknowledged by all of the other parts.

The representation of the Abandoned Baby kept shifting over time, becoming brighter and more complex. Maria found an old photograph of herself and used it in a representation she referred to as the "original injured child." She pasted the photograph on a small box and put several images of the remaining wounded child parts in it.

This (now-composite) injured child had three primary resources: her adult self, which was learning to become a more nurturing inner parent figure; me (her therapist); and Strawberry. With the love of all three, the injured child became brighter and happier over time.

At a later point, Maria made a composite of the injured child (now called by her natural name) and Strawberry, indicating that the boundary between them had become more permeable. She also worked with representations of the adult self (which also evolved with time) and a core spiritual self, which she called The Ancient One.

As so often happens, Maria's parts work dropped into the background as the parts became more integrated. Her adult self took on more and more of the flavor of Sweet Innocence as Maria let go of her defenses. This was supported by my mirroring in therapy, by Strawberry, and by her ability to appropriately defend herself both in her inner and outer worlds. We could say Maria evolved from a stone child to a sweet child to a more loving adult. Parts work wasn't the only factor in Maria's healing, but it was an important one.

## Becoming your own best mother

The renowned Jungian analyst and author Marion Woodman said, "Children who are not loved in their very beingness do not know how to love themselves. As adults, they have to learn to nourish, to mother their own lost child."

This learning happens in stages. We, in essence, grow into the job. Just as a woman doesn't automatically know how to mother offspring but her instincts and her heart can be awakened, so it is with our own capacity to bond with and actively "mother" the child states inside us.

It may feel awkward at first, and there may be any number of obstacles. One of the first that may come up is a feeling of inadequacy. If you weren't well mothered, you can easily feel that you haven't a clue how to do it. You're uncomfortable, you don't know what to say or do, and you feel phony trying what doesn't come naturally. This is enough to stop you right here.

Second, if you succeed in making an authentic connection with the undermothered parts within yourself, you may be struck by a sense of guilt that you have inadvertently continued the abandonment by not showing up earlier. No one likes to feel the sharp pain of causing harm to another.

And just as I've mentioned earlier that a mother may unconsciously keep a distance from a child so as not to arouse her own hurt, you may feel that opening up the locked-away pain in your heart is too high a price to pay for reconnecting with child parts inside you.

In addition to the pain, we fear being taken over. When we've pushed any aspect of us into the unconscious, we often fear that if we open to it, it will be overwhelming. (This is true of repressed anger, sadness, sexuality, and so on.) In a similar manner, we may fear that the needs of our inner child may be more than we are equipped to deal with and will overwhelm us or take over.

To the extent that you are still unconsciously identified with the undermothered child (and usually we are for a long time), you won't experience yourself as an abundant source with much to give but rather as someone who's dry and depleted. You may think, *I don't have enough for myself. How can I nurture someone else?*

> ➤ Which of the following obstacles can you recognize in yourself?
>   - feeling you don't know how to mother
>   - guilt about not showing up earlier
>   - self-protection, not wanting to feel your own hurt
>   - fear of everything that has been repressed
>   - feeling that you don't have enough to give
>
> ➤ What might help you work through these?

The most important step in becoming your own best mother is to move beyond your inadequacies, fears, and defenses and let your heart soften. The heart that is open is a heart that can love.

Your inner child will help you. A child is like a "love bank": The more you put in, the more you get back. Children are innately loving, so as you extend even a trickle of love to the unloved child within you, usually that child will extend love back. It is often shocking when first making contact with orphaned and exiled parts of us how receptive they are and how pure their little child hearts are.

This is not always the case, for sometimes an inner child will initially respond with mistrust. Just as a child who has been hurt or abandoned too many times by Mother will not open his arms to her, the inner child may react similarly. If this is the case, persist in your efforts to reach out to this child the best you can, realizing that it takes time to build trust.

As you become more nurturing to yourself, it may kick up reactions inside that parallel something in your early environment. For example, if your father couldn't tolerate anyone being "coddled" or treated gently, then when you start to treat yourself in a really caring, gentle manner, you may hear some internal self-talk that sounds an awful lot like Dad. You'll need to be on the lookout and recognize when the feelings and reactions inside are not really your own. Learn to stand behind the Good Mother that is slowly developing inside you.

Many women who were undermothered and who choose to become biological mothers have struggled with these internal forces and made a commitment on a deep soul level not to abandon their children as they were abandoned. They go to great lengths to learn how to become good mothers, looking for models to follow, reading books, asking for help. They don't expect to automatically know how to do it.

In a similar way, in re-parenting ourselves, we can make a commitment to learning and developing in ways that may not feel natural to us at first. We can look for models, read books, and ask for help. We can also call upon capacities already within us that we haven't used this way before. Many who have been undermothered have paradoxically taken on the job of nurturing and caretaking others, such as a sibling or mate. In helping clients develop a nurturing parent inside themselves, one therapeutic approach, the Developmental Needs Meeting Strategy, has clients recall a time they were nurturing to another and use that as a basis for creating a nurturing parent within themselves. You can try this for yourself.

Remember a time when you felt nurturing or protective of another or were actually involved in caregiving. Bring this feeling all the way through you. Intensify it. You may have muted your natural inclinations then, but give them an extra boost now. Feel yourself as a nurturing adult who can mother the undernurtured child within. How do you feel this in your body? Take an inner snapshot of you in this role, so you have an image to call upon later.

Learning to check in with the child may require effort at first, but it can become a more automatic and integral part of life. Be aware of the energy you initially bring to this. You don't want to repeat the feeling tone of a resentful mother here. Your child is a joy, not a burden.

Fortunately, becoming a good mother to your inner child(ren) is innately reinforcing. One woman reported that it boosted her self-esteem. It feels good to be attentive and loving, and once the relationship is well established, there's lots of love coming back from the child.

## Creating a safe place for the child

Healing begins with finding the parts that we've lost contact with, which, within the context of this book, are child parts. Many of these are child parts that split off and dissociated because it wasn't safe for them. These vulnerable child parts need to know that they are safe with you now and that the situation is different.

Nancy Napier, who works with self-hypnotic states (which are simply states of deep relaxation and receptivity), writes in her book *Reclaiming Your Self*, "Bringing the child into the present is an important part of the process. In the timeless unconscious, the child continues to experience the original childhood environment as if it were the present. When current situations link back to that dysfunctional environment, the child doesn't realize that he or she lives with you, now, in a different place."[76]

You have to give extra attention to safety to keep the child anchored in the present. By establishing a strong, nurturing relationship between child states and a loving inner parent, the child can get unstuck from the past and have a happy home life. This happens as we listen respectfully and with empathy to the child parts and give them avenues for expressing themselves, such as through art or the use of dialogues.

You might set aside a time to dialogue with your inner child states about what they need to feel safe.

## Time together

Once you bring the child out of the traumatic past (which sometimes happens very easily), you can create a more child-friendly environment now.

This may involve a mix of time simply dialoguing with this child aspect or being together in an easy relaxed way and doing things that you know this child enjoys. If the child in you likes being outdoors, make sure you get some time outside. Or maybe horseback riding or roller skating feel nurturing. Sometimes we blend with the child when we're doing these activities, but often you will also feel your adult self present. Having the adult around is good in terms of supervision and also in terms of building relationship and re-parenting.

Another way that is just as effective is to create time in your imagination to meet the child's needs. One woman spends time with each of her three inner kids daily, treating them much as she would actual children those ages. She bathes and holds the baby and takes the teenager shopping. Each of the inner children can be seen going through the normal developmental stages that would have occurred in a stable, loving home. They are healing under her good-mother care.

You can heal the neglect of your childhood by caring for your inner children now.

## Working with Good Mother messages

In the first chapter, I offered a list of ten Good Mother messages, repeated below. These can help establish you as a caring mother to any child within you. I encourage you to find some way that helps you feel the child's presence (whether working with a doll or picture or representation) and say these statements aloud. Notice if any are more evocative than others for the child and which are most difficult for you. These are the ones you will want to concentrate on.

Often when something is new for us, we need to step into it slowly, and this is true when dealing with positive states that are unfamiliar. We need to get used to them and give them a chance to become threaded into us and absorbed, so give this exercise plenty of time and space. By feeling a positive experience really fully, you in essence "install" it into your reservoir of resources. Tune in to your body and see how it responds to each message. You'll want to work in a relaxed state where you are more receptive and able to notice your reactions.

🍃 I'm glad that you're here.

🍃 I see you.

🍃 You are special to me.

🍃 I respect you.

🍃 I love you.

🍃 Your needs are important to me. You can turn to me for help.

🍃 I am here for you. I'll make time for you.

🍃 I'll keep you safe.

🍃 You can rest in me.

🍃 I enjoy you. You brighten my heart.

Don't stop here. You can also create your own Good Mother messages. If you do this in conjunction with specific inner children, they will be even more on target. Ask these child states what they want to hear.

Another exercise is to create statements from the child's voice that are reassuring. Here are some examples:

🍃 Mommy loves to give to me and to help me.

🍃 Mommy is available, ready when I need something.

🍃 Mommy is really proud of me.

🍃 Mommy really likes me!

Please don't think of these as a onetime experience. The more frequently and deeply you work with them, the more they can take hold within you and become part of a new foundation.

---

### A letter to your child (an exercise)

Set aside some uninterrupted time and create a soothing atmosphere to do some inner work. (This might involve finding the right background music, lighting a candle, turning off your phone, or going to a special place.) After a short, centering meditation, compose a letter to your inner child (if you haven't differentiated several child states) or to a particular inner child or your child at a particular age. Write either from your normal adult state or, if you can access it, from the place in you that can be a nurturing parent to this child. Tell this child how you feel about what she or he has been through. If it feels appropriate and genuine to include some of the Good Mother messages, do.

---

## Healing the unloved child

For most who are undermothered, the major focus of re-parenting will be healing the unloved child. There are other needs, of course—for guidance, encouragement, protection, anchoring—and providing these can be part of healing the unloved child, but first and foremost it is a matter of offering a warm, caring connection. This child, like every child, needs to be loved.

One inner child told me she just needed to be held, with no agenda and no time limit. She needed the "envelope" of a Good Mommy. Some of the infant states are very fragile and delicate and need very gentle holding so they can develop and mature.

In expressing nurturance toward an inner child, it is helpful to have an outer representation that you can have physical contact with. You might use a doll or stuffed animal to represent a younger self. Soft objects are the nicest to hold and stroke, and they absorb your tears.

Sometimes people sleep with a doll or carry it in a snuggly baby holder. Most will at least hold or talk to a representation of this kind.

Not infrequently people first meet an inner child who is somewhere in the three-to-six-year age range, yet at some point an infant will show up. Working with the infant self often brings up the most painful feelings of all. Even though you may be going backward in terms of age, working through these primal wounds is a sign of your strength.

## Changing your mind

Giving Good Mother messages to your inner child, receiving Good Mother messages from others, and really cultivating the Good Mother within yourself does more than just satisfy needs of your inner child. It quite literally changes your mind. It changes your structure, your beliefs about yourself and the world.

Over time, the Good Mother voice you have cultivated can replace the Critical Parent voice that is a major filter in most people's minds. If you are stuck in Critical Parent, then you will be that way (at least in your mind) with others. You'll be impatient and judgmental and not really able to open your heart to them. Of course you'll also be this way with yourself—and you likely know what that is like. Wouldn't it be much nicer to have a loving filter that you see the world through?

So there are many benefits to opening up to Good Mother energy. The work is time consuming but worth it. Changing the inner atmosphere of your mind is the biggest remodel job you can take on.

# 11.

# More Healing Steps and Practical Strategies

I've given you many options for working with your mother wound, but I would be remiss if I didn't include this proactive approach built on needs we've identified. Consider the following:

- Not everyone is going to be lucky enough to find someone who is willing to serve as a replacement for the Good Mother they missed in childhood.

- Not everyone has a partner who wants a conscious relationship and is willing to let that relationship be a place to work on childhood wounds and unmet needs.

- Not everyone is going to be drawn to the Great Mother or to working on the archetypal realm.

- Not everyone has the resources, commitment, or inclination to do psychotherapy.

- Not everyone is comfortable working with the child within.

- *But everyone can,* in addition to any of the above, employ the perspective of this chapter to proactively identify and meet needs that are left over from childhood.

### Identifying specific "holes"

For the undermothered child, the hole where Mom should have been can feel as big as the universe. When we come back to it as an adult, we may feel that there is no way to fill it—that it's unfillable.

It is essential to see through this feeling and realize that the hole *can* be filled. It helps when we remember that this spot in our psyche is simply a place where pieces of ourselves have not yet filled in because they didn't have the support they needed. It is not an endless abyss but rather is made up of specific holes where the functions of the Good Mother were not met. Between these spaces is dry land! Despite what was missing, there are places where your development was supported and consequently there are pieces of yourself that are solid and real. It's important to feel what is there as well as what is still missing or underdeveloped.

Here is a list of ten needs we all had as children. You'll notice a great deal of overlap with the ten functions of the Good Mother listed in chapter 2.

- To feel that you belong somewhere and are part of the larger web of life

- To attach to others in a secure way and know it is safe to be vulnerable and show your needs

- To be seen for who you are and have your feelings met (mirroring)

- To have help and guidance that is calibrated to your needs

- To receive encouragement and support, to feel that someone is behind you

- To have others serve as a model for you and teach you skills that you need to succeed

- To have needs met in a timely way and to be comforted and soothed when you are upset, thus establishing an ability to soothe yourself and bring your system back into balance (self-regulation)

🐾 To have adequate protection so that you are safe and are not overwhelmed

🐾 To be treated in a way that communicates respect (for your boundaries, needs, feelings, and so on)

🐾 To feel loved and cared for

Another universal need is to feel valued, but I did not include this as a separate item because I think the sense of value is the result of, and comes with, all of these. Value comes when we feel that we belong and are part of a positively valued group. Value comes with secure attachment. Value comes with positive mirroring that helps us know and accept all parts of ourselves. When others take time to guide, support, and encourage us, it communicates that they value us. When others provide appropriate protection and want to keep us safe, it tells us that we are precious to them. Likewise, when people treat us with respect, it helps build a sense of value. And certainly being loved gives us a sense of being lovable and having value.

---

**Identifying your needs (an exercise)**

Look at the list of ten needs above. For each need, consider how well it was fulfilled in your childhood and where you are now with it. If it helps to use a numerical rating system, here is one you can use:

    1 – strongly unfulfilled
    2 – somewhat unfulfilled
    3 – somewhat fulfilled
    4 – quite fulfilled

However you choose to do the exercise, the goal is to end up with a list of needs that are still active.

## Taking a proactive approach

Rather than look back at an absent mother and get caught in the feelings of the unfillable hole, it is more fruitful to step back from the feelings, assess what specific holes need to be filled, and responsibly go after what you need in each of these areas.

In *Growing Up Again: Parenting Ourselves, Parenting Our Children,* authors Jean Illsley Clarke and Connie Dawson talk about healing one hole at a time. "There is no quick fix," they write. "There is no magical, sudden way to borrow the needed skills and to reclaim our self-confidence and self-esteem. We must do it ourselves step by step; we must build it from within." [77]

Building it starts with identifying what we need. So, for example, if you know you never had much encouragement and you recognize that you often avoid doing things that are new or that you haven't developed skills for, you might ask yourself, "What do I need for support? Do I need someone to mentor me? Do I need some cheerleading? How can I work on developing more self-support?"

If you feel disconnected and as if you don't belong anywhere, you could look for places to develop relationships and eventually experience a sense of belonging. You might also consider how work or volunteer activities can give you a place in the web.

Many of these will have both an outer and inner level. So, for example, if you feel as if you'd benefit from more love, you can consider both how to cultivate loving relationships and ways to nurture your own self-love.

The point I want to make is that we can be proactive. In general, I think there are three ways we can go after the pieces that we've missed:

- We can identify what we need and ask for it directly.

- We can look for people and situations where whatever we seek is easily found (e.g., a situation in which safe touch is plentiful).

- We can provide ourselves with what was missing.

I find that when I am specific in my needs with others, asking precisely for what I want (in a nondemanding way), it works quite well. Sometimes I even give people their "lines" (often making a joke about it) and then ask that they use them only if they can do so sincerely. Often people respond by saying, "Absolutely I can say that," and then repeat what I've asked to hear. When others start off in a direction that's not helpful, I gently try to steer them to what I'm looking for. So I might, for example, tell someone this isn't the time when I want to hear their critique of my next book idea and all the challenges that might come with it; right now I need their support. I might say something like, "I want you to say it's an exciting idea and you're behind me."

If we can tell people when we want to be held, when we need our feelings mirrored, when we need verbal support, and so on, we won't feel so powerless. Another advantage is that we don't look like "unfillable" holes to other people, who will likely respond with some kind of pulling away from what is perceived as endless need. Specific needs are generally less threatening and overwhelming to everyone.

### The hole of support

The hole of support is one of the most common in children of emotionally disengaged parents. Often we didn't have a person who provided support for our efforts and support for us when our efforts failed. There was no one jumping up and down, saying, "Yes, you can do this!" or "I'm behind you." In the desired situation, that person is the mother, joined by the father and others as well. Without people who communicate that they believe in us, it is harder to believe in ourselves.

This lack of support often means that our confidence doesn't develop normally or fully. We can feel as if we are missing a piece—and we are! We're missing something inside us that develops when a child receives consistent support. We're missing our sense of capacity and inner support. This leaves us feeling intimidated, inadequate, and insecure. When we feel the hole of support, we say things to ourselves like, "It's too big. I don't think I can do it," or "I feel so alone with this."

Issues of support often come up when we are tackling something new and the outcome is not guaranteed, or when we come up against challenges. We often need support when we have a "failure" of some sort.

Rather than blame yourself for your lack of confidence and wonder why you can't just push ahead like others seem to do, it may be helpful to take a look at how much support you had growing up. I'm going to keep the questions broad so you can answer them with whatever parental figures you had.

> ➤ How often did a parent come to any performances or events you were involved in? What did they say afterward? What did their body language convey? Did it feel supportive that they came?

> ➤ How did your parents respond to your accomplishments? Were your achievements acknowledged and celebrated?

> ➤ Apart from accomplishments, did you have a sense of parental support just for being you and for the inherent challenges of growing up?

> ➤ How did your parents respond to feelings of fear, insecurity, or inadequacy? What about times you were a little down and just needed to know that someone cared?

> ➤ Did you have a sense that there was a parental figure you could go to in times of need?

As with almost any area we explore, we see the family legacy at play. We reject or fail to support in ourselves and our children what was not supported by our parents, which, in turn, generally wasn't supported by theirs. We can break this chain by consciously deciding to.

## Getting support now

If you want to reverse a pattern of inadequate support, you need to first examine what your needs are and commit to building more support. You will also want to notice how well you take in support when it is offered. Often when we didn't receive much when we were young, our ability to receive gets blocked by defenses that we developed.

There are many approaches to bolstering your sense of support both in the self-help literature and therapy. Here's my list of helpful strategies:

### Ask for support from others.

This is not an optional skill but an essential one. You must be able to ask for support and encouragement in whatever form you need from people who have a decent chance of providing it.

### Learn to access others even when they're not there.

When others aren't available, you can take the process inside. You can do this either as internal dialogue or as a dialogue that shows up in your journal. If you are journaling, simply imagine what that person would say. You can do this with anyone, including a Good Mommy figure or imagined guide or Higher Self.

### Find supportive structures.

Get creative about collecting or developing supportive structures, including support groups, classes, work groups, an exercise buddy, or whatever would be helpful in a particular situation. Consider how you can set up a series of goals and rewards and what routines and learning situations can help you.

### Step away from your feelings and get objective.

Remind yourself of your actual capacities. The sense that you don't have enough support is, in the end, only a feeling. As a feeling, it can limit you, but only if you are paying more attention to that feeling than to your capacities to meet a situation.

### Support your inner child.

Since often it is an inner child state that gets caught in feelings of fear and insecurity, you can step into your own Good Mother and dialogue with the child, listening to her fears, providing empathy, holding, and reassurance.

### Say nice things to yourself.

Notice if you're repeating deflating messages to yourself and replace these with positive statements. Ask yourself, "What would a Good Mother say in this situation?" Here are some statements you might work with:

- 🍂 I have faith in you.

- 🍂 I know you can do this.

- 🍂 I'm behind you, whatever happens.

### Make it real through imagery.

Imagine having the support you need. Feel this as vividly as possible. See yourself moving easily through whatever feels challenging.

### Feel the fear and do it anyway.

If there is a particular task that is difficult, it may help to dive into it. The engagement itself and any progress you make can provide support. If fear leads you to back down and cave in, the fear has won, and will be used again.

### Access the support of your body.

Not everyone feels their body as a resource, but if you can, it's a great asset. For example, sensing your bones can provide a sense of solidity. There may be other subtle cues you can use as well, like pressing your lips together. Feeling your muscles can feel good, and getting some exercise may help break the spell of inadequacy.

### Reach to Spirit for help.

Millions of people turn to Spirit for help in times of need. This may take the form of spiritual beings outside yourself or contacting the part of your own being that is far beyond what you normally experience. I can say unequivocally that support is definitely available.

For the undermothered, support is often an issue that requires continued attention. It is worth the effort it takes, however. As we learn to seek out and take in external support and slowly develop more internal support, we find that we move forward with more ease. There aren't the same limits then, and life becomes less of a struggle.

## A sense of confidence

What is confidence, and where does it come from? Confidence is not all or nothing, but rather something we feel more of or less of in different areas of our lives. As adults, we may feel confident about our relationship skills but not our computer skills or confident in our decision making but not in our ability to aggressively go after what we want.

I've observed that for some people confidence is more closely associated with doing (and is dependent on their skills and performance), while for others it is related more to their felt security with others. My suspicion is that confidence gets tied up with doing when parents put a lot of emphasis on competence. When children are not shamed for undeveloped skills but rather are loved quite fully just for being who they are, then competence becomes less important. The secure person simply says, "I don't know how to do that," and looks on with curiosity. A child's competence at whatever level needs to be mirrored for the child to take that into his identity; otherwise the child will often feel inadequate.

Although it would be a mistake to make our confidence as an adult dependent on how others feel about us (just as it is a mistake to make it dependent on how well we perform), having a secure attachment serves as a foundation for a child's sense of confidence. A secure attachment gives you a place in the world, the sense that someone values and is invested in you, and the sense that you have a right to be here and take up space. One way to define confidence is as the courage to show up and express yourself. That's easier when others have supported this.

We can look at our list of needs and say confidence comes with almost all of them. It comes when we feel wanted and are an accepted part of a larger group that we feel good about. It comes when we are seen and accepted for who we are and when we are treated with respect. When others encourage and praise us, it builds confidence. When we know we'll have the help and support we need, it builds confidence. When we can regulate our own physiology, our ups and downs, and bring ourselves back to balance, this gives steadiness and confidence.

You can ask your inner child what he or she needs to develop more confidence. One such child said she needed to feel safe, to feel liked, to have someone excited about what she could do, and to have someone see her strength.

What do you need to develop more confidence?

## Navigating the world of emotions

Humans naturally live in the world of emotions, but for some who are undermothered, this world is more uncomfortable than not. Learning to navigate these waters is an important part of functioning successfully in the world and being a full human being.

John Bradshaw explains how many get cut off from this world: "Children growing up in dysfunctional families are taught to inhibit the expression of emotion in three ways: first, by not being responded to or mirrored, literally not being seen; second, by having no healthy models for naming and expressing emotion; and third, by actually being shamed and/or punished for expressing emotion." [78] He continues, "The earlier the emotions are inhibited, the deeper the damage." [79]

When emotions have been cut off in this way, becoming part of the world of emotion may require significant learning. We have to break the spell of our own "still face" and become transparent. This may be harder to do with some emotions than others. The feelings that our parents had a particularly hard time tolerating will usually be the ones that we have the hardest time tolerating if we have not yet healed this.

**Expanding your repertoire (an exercise)**

➤ Which of the following emotions are hardest for you to accept and express?

- hurt
- sadness
- joy
- anger
- fear
- vulnerability
- pride
- bewilderment
- hatred
- desire
- love
- awe
- disappointment
- remorse
- envy
- jealousy
- confidence
- happiness

➤ Which were hardest for each of your parental figures?

➤ Using this list as a jumping-off point, make a list of emotions that you want to add to your emotional palette.

➤ For each of the emotions you have just named, write about what would support you in developing it.

Just as we can be proactive with the other deficits identified in this chapter, we can be proactive in claiming or reclaiming emotions we have not been able to easily express. For example, perhaps in your family of origin, there was no room for you to show disappointment, and you notice that you are still shy about expressing it. It might help to select a trusted person, share some disappointments, and ask for validation. Ask to have the disappointment mirrored and normalized. An example of normalizing might be, "Of course that would be hard! I would be disappointed, too." If you were shamed in the past for showing disappointment, this could be a powerful corrective experience.

## Emotional style and caretaking patterns

Remember that many who are undermothered will need to work on continuing to get in touch with their feelings. When Mother didn't notice or respond to feelings, we often don't have a strong connection with them ourselves. We may even have learned to turn them off in order to keep what thread of connection we felt with Mother.

Our individual style, whether we suppress feelings or exaggerate them to get attention, generally develops in response to our caretaker's style. It makes sense that when caretakers are consistently uninterested in a child's feelings or act punitively toward the child for expressing feelings, children learn to suppress their emotions. We can also see how when caregivers are sometimes responsive in an attuned way and other times just don't get it, children are more likely to exaggerate feelings in order to get help, which is what the research finds.[80]

Take a moment to reflect on this.

> ➤ Are you more likely to hide your feelings out of fear of rejection or to "whip them up" when you want a response from someone?

> ➤ If you do some of both, which feelings or in which
> circumstances do you tend to conceal your feelings,
> and when do you let them get really big? What do you
> expect will happen when you let your feelings get big?

## A place in the web

Many who did not experience a strong connection with their mother also feel a lack of connection with other family members or with the family as a whole. That leaves a hole, something missing. We rely on family to connect us with the world in a meaningful way by giving us any number of things: a port in the storm, a sense of belonging, identity, support. We look to family to find a place where we are known and held.

If you have your own mate and/or children now, this may help compensate for the earlier disconnection, but what if you have only your family of origin, to which you feel so thinly tethered? What if you have no place that is home in the sense of tribe or family?

The nuclear family has taken on disproportionate importance as the larger sense of tribe or community has diminished in Western culture. In some cultures, the whole village takes on the role of family, but here we're talking about a very limited number of individuals. Instead of being connected by dozens or hundreds of threads, we're held by half a dozen—maybe even only one or two. That is not enough to sustain a healthy sense of connection and belonging.

What is the solution? To build additional strands of connection and belonging. Some of the primary ways we do this are through the following:

- A circle of close friends may serve as a "family of
  choice," being there in times of need and celebrating
  important passages in our lives with us.

- Ties to groups help give us a place in the web of life. These may be interest groups, healing groups, social groups, or any other. For some, their community is one whose interactions take place across the World Wide Web. While a virtual community alone may miss some important aspects, it does provide a sense of connection that is meaningful to many.

- Meaningful work (volunteer or paid) gives us a place and purpose in the world.

- Ties to places anchor us in a physical way to the planet, so that we're not simply wanderers or "lost in space." This could be a sense of connection with your home or the area surrounding your home. Many people feel a strong connection with the land around them.

## Showing up and being seen

Often when we're not mirrored, we lose contact with parts of ourselves. It's a journey to recover these, a journey that involves being seen now. Of course seeing yourself is part of it, and any kind of self-exploration will help, but having others see and acknowledge these lost parts helps cement them in place.

While the invisibility may have started with parents too busy, too checked out, or not capable of really seeing you, it may be maintained by our own habits and a certain turning away from the world. Often to survive the emotional barrenness of emotionally absent parents or any early environment that did not feel welcoming, we turn into ourselves. Rather than reach out in relationships, we withdraw. Part of healing is coming out of the cloister and back into the world.

In expanding your opportunities to be seen, you might consider expressive and even performance activities, such as theater, group singing, and dance. My mother is a very conventional woman who shows little of herself, and I have found it very freeing to participate in activities that pull me out of a similar tendency to hold back, activities where people are spontaneous and uninhibited.

Some groups provide an opportunity for a person to have the stage (the group's full attention) for a moment and just be seen. The person in the center can express anything he or she wants. Often what is most healing is simply to be transparent in that moment, showing true feelings.

## Embracing your needs

When it comes to our needs, we tend to adopt the attitude our parents had toward them, at least initially. So, for example, if your mother was impatient with your needs or rejecting, you'll tend to have little tolerance yourself. I remember a time in my own therapy when I had just expressed a fair amount of neediness and suddenly felt very apologetic. I was, in essence, rolling my eyes as if to say, *This is way too much!* Fortunately, I noticed it and recognized it as a hand-me-down from my parents. "I'm glad you caught that," my therapist told me, "because I don't feel that way at all."

For many whose needs were not met in their early years, needs feel humiliating and dangerous. One woman disclosed that putting herself in a dependent position vis-à-vis another felt like handing them a knife to cut her throat. Feeling dependent was associated with feeling raw and unprotected and about to get clobbered.

Moving through this is not easy. We need to learn that it is not dangerous now and that we can be met, including by people who *want* to meet our needs! Learning this involves some risk, because we won't know until we try. That risk can be hard to tolerate.

New experience can help change old beliefs. When our needs are ignored when we're young, we often feel rejected for having needs. This can lead to a belief that our needs are too much or that our needs will drive others away. The belief gets dismantled by showing our needs and having them met.

It's helpful if you can start by reaching out in small ways to people who are safe. The risk is less this way, and you can slowly build your tolerance for the vulnerability as well as a reservoir of experiences where your needs were met.

For those with a self-sufficient style, it's a long journey from "I'll do it myself" to "I'm so happy for your help." It means learning that your needs can actually be the place where others are responsive to you.

Knowing your needs and being able to express them is an important developmental achievement that supports intimacy, authors Jett Psaris and Marlena Lyons acknowledge in their book *Undefended Love*. Yet it's not the whole story. We want to feel okay even when our needs aren't met by partners. As Psaris and Lyons note, "The earlier the unresolved need, the less capable we are as adults of sustaining our sense of well-being when that need is not fulfilled by another."[81] When our early dependency needs weren't met as infants, our consciousness often fractured in that moment. We didn't have the resources or maturity to "hold it together," meaning to hold ourselves together. That intolerable rawness and sensitivity around need comes from these very early injuries.

It can be embarrassing to expose these unpolished aspects of ourselves, but it is part of the process. We bring to our intimate relationships everything we didn't work through or complete in childhood. From the perspective of those who see relationship as a path of growth, that is a blessing.

To explore where you are in your healing journey, consider the following questions:

> ➤ How do you feel about having needs? Can you see
>   how this mirrors how early caregivers felt about and
>   responded to your needs?

> Do you generally expect that others will be available when you need them, or do you carry more sense of deprivation in relation to this?

> Which of your needs is hardest to express?

> Can you expose a need, have it only partially filled, and be okay with that? Do you have room to, in essence, "hold" your needs rather than pass them off like a hot potato or suppress them altogether?

## Practicing good self-care

As I mentioned above, we tend to treat ourselves as we have been treated. For some this leads to a marked lack of good self-care. Sometimes this comes out of lack of awareness, other times from aversion. One woman told me that she had the distinct feeling "I hate taking care of you" when prompted to start paying attention to her skin. She would wait until her skin was cracking before applying moisturizing lotion. Another came to see me wearing no socks on a snowy day. She didn't notice that her feet were cold.

Other times we don't want to take care of ourselves because we secretly want others to take care of us. I've heard the belief "If I take care of my needs, then no one else will, and I'll never be taken care of by another." One woman told me that she would only get holding if she fell apart (so meeting her own needs was in opposition to getting holding).

It's not true that meeting our own needs is exclusive of having needs met by others. I find that in my social circle, I prefer meeting the needs of friends who show that they care about themselves. Meeting some of your own needs makes you less dependent and clingy. It models how you want others to treat you.

Most important, practicing good self-care gives a different message to your system. It says, "I care about you. You are important." For a child of neglect, this message is medicine.

> What are the ways that you neglect your physical or emotional well-being? (Be as detailed as you can.) What are you willing to do to change this pattern? You might also think of ways you can do a better job in areas you are not currently neglecting.

> Create a list of things you can do when you need to feel nurtured. Look for healthy things, perhaps things a Good Mother would suggest or provide, like a hot bath, a foot rub, curling up in a comfy chair with a comforter and a good book, or making a pot of soup or a nourishing hot drink.

## Cultivating a capacity for intimacy

Intimacy requires emotional openness, a willingness to see and be seen, and letting your needs be a place where you are met. This will be challenging if you haven't worked through the residues left by unresponsive parenting, but it is worth working toward. Although you may have carried deep disappointment about relationships over many years, you also likely carry a deep longing, and you can use this longing to help propel you forward when you're hanging back, caught in a self-protective posture.

One way of proactively working with this is to think about what you do to foster intimacy. What are the "attachment behaviors" that are part of your repertoire, and how can you increase these. Consider the following:

> Can you accept comfort at times of threat or when in distress? (This is an "attachment behavior.")

> How do you respond when someone reaches out to you? Can you allow someone to need you?

> Can you touch in caring ways? Sustain intimate eye contact?

> ➤ During lovemaking, can you keep emotional contact?

> ➤ What fears and defenses come up when you get really close to a partner?

One therapist reports that when a couple is able to increase their attachment bond, it helps each partner self-regulate and resolves some of their individual problems. For those with a self-reliant style, the task is to wake up the attachment system, which can then function more normally, as nature intended it. Consider what you can do to cultivate the capacities that allow for intimacy.

## Protecting what is precious

As we've learned, one of the functions of the Good Mother is to provide a safe place, a protected environment in which her child can grow and blossom. We continue to need this as an adult. We need an environment that safely and comfortably holds us and that feels nourishing. Just as the Good Mother provides this for the infant, we must learn to provide it for ourselves as adults.

There are several aspects to a holding environment and the sense of safe, protected space. One is our home, where we live. Does your home feel both safe and nourishing? Is it a place you like to be? What happens when you move one level farther out to the surrounding area? Do you feel at home in your neighborhood?

How about boundaries, both as it relates to others touching your body and to psychological boundaries? Can you keep others at the right distance? Do you let others intrude on your privacy or in your psychic space, with nosy questions and unwanted advice? If someone moves into your personal space either physically or emotionally in a way you don't want, can you push them back to a more comfortable distance?

Boundaries will generally be more difficult for those who have had intrusive parents and whose families were enmeshed rather than emotionally disengaged, but even families that are emotionally distant can have boundary violations. In order to let out the more hidden and vulnerable parts of you, it's essential that you feel you can protect yourself as needed.

Just as the Good Mother arranges the environment for the young child so that nothing will be experienced as harsh or invasive and what the child needs is available, part of cherishing ourselves is to pay attention to what is too much and what is just right for us. So, for example, it is knowing what is too much social contact, what is not enough, and what is most satisfying. Obviously it's not just a matter of quantity but quality, so we look at what kinds of contact are satisfying and what is not and then adjust our lives accordingly. Here the protection role and modulation role are combined. Modulation is making things just right. Not too much and not too little.

Here are some questions to help you assess how well you are fulfilling the Good Mother roles of protector and modulator:

> Where in your life, if anywhere, are you not protecting what is precious in you?

> If you were creating a "holding" that was just right for you, what would be different than it currently is? Consider as many levels as you can, including the physical environment, social environment, and emotional environment.

### Finding your power

It's hard to be successful in life when you don't have your full power. Without your power, you're hindered in your attempts to compete on the many stages of life, whether the athletic field, the marketplace, or even the dating arena. Therapists sometimes refer to the sense of power as self-efficacy or a sense of "agency" (as in being an agent acting on your environment). Often we think of this in terms of the power to change our circumstances, but it is also empowering to know that we can change our internal experience, such as our mental patterns or our mood. When you know you can change things, you are no longer a victim.

There are an untold number of ways you can increase your sense of empowerment, including:

- Developing communication skills that help you advocate for your needs.

- Finding the power to say no (through assertiveness training or self-defense classes, for instance).

- Finding situations where you can make a difference and minimizing situations where you can't. Some situations are inherently disempowering.

- Noticing when you do have an effect on a situation. You can't grow your sense of power if you keep overlooking times when you are effective. You must take in experiences of success so they get braided into your self-concept.

- Learning to change your self-talk. Self-talk is the running dialogue you have in your head about things, and especially about yourself. There are classes, books, and articles that can help you move from a pattern of negative assessment and commentary to something more positive, compassionate, and objective.

- Finding the power in your body. This doesn't mean bodybuilding, although it could include that, but more coming into your body—what many would call "embodiment." Body-centered therapies can help with this, as can anything that increases your awareness of your body, such as a good yoga practice.

- Working through the issues that have blocked your power, utilizing avenues such as psychotherapy.

- Learning how to locate resources to help with specific needs. Being empowered doesn't mean you have to do everything all by yourself. Think of the CEOs of the world!

## Stepping out of deprivation consciousness

Mother is our first environment, and how we experience her has great impact on how we subsequently experience the world and what we expect from it. If Mother was not responsive to our early needs, we generally don't expect the world to be; if Mother was not welcoming, we don't perceive the world as welcoming. In fact, a major part of healing is seeing that the world is not the same as Mother, changing both our perceptions and our relationship with it.

I have found many who were undernurtured as children to have what might be called *deprivation consciousness*. It is a sense of lack that is carried within and becomes the unconscious filter through which we receive experience. We might go so far as to say some of us create a "deprivation story" that becomes the repeating theme of our life. A deprivation story is filled with thoughts such as "There's never enough for me" or "I'll never get what I want." Often this will be in contrast with how you see others. It's as if you're the last baby in the row at the orphanage, and they always run out before they get to you.

If you resonate with this sense of deprivation, consider the following:

➤ What's the flavor of the deprivation you feel? Is there an image or a metaphor that captures it?

➤ Can you see how this flavor has run through your life?

Only after you metabolize the pain in the experiences that generated this story will you be able to eventually let go of the story and have a different experience.

As part of that process, you may also want to do some exploration of any barriers that may be present to having a different experience now. Try to imagine what abundance would feel like. Where does it rub up against self-images that block it? How would it change your sense of you to feel there is plenty rather than not enough?

When we experience something totally unfamiliar, it can bring a sense of shock at first. If you've essentially never had good support and then have someone who behaves in a totally supportive way with you, you may find yourself feeling rather disoriented, wondering if this is real. Think of the people who win the lottery, gain instant riches, but a few years later are back at the level they were beforehand. That instant and drastic change wasn't ever integrated.

> Can you think of a time when your sense of deprivation was challenged by something quite contrary to it?

> List five examples of times when you had everything you needed or more than you could wish for. What did that feel like?

Sometimes the sense of deprivation is deeply branded into our psyche, but we try to displace it by steeping ourselves in symbols of abundance. This may be preferable to the earlier experience, but even better still is when the old imprint dissolves and we leave deprivation consciousness altogether. Then, even in the midst of a very ordinary life, we feel rich.

**Counting your blessings exercise**

At the beginning of the chapter, I said that between the holes is dry land; between the deficits and places we are underdeveloped are places where we have what we need. Part of empowerment and stepping out of deprivation consciousness is being solidly anchored in our strengths and resources. We'll look at this as three different lists, one dealing with capacities that you have developed, the second as assets or blessings in your life, and third (perhaps the hardest) of positive things about your childhood.

Make a list of twenty capacities that you have developed. Here are some examples:

- I know how to be a good friend and provide support to others.

- I am resourceful and know how to get the information I need.

- I am compassionate with myself as well as others (maybe not all the time but a good deal of the time).

- I have learned to recognize my feelings and can verbalize them rather than simply act them out.

- I am able to feel my own preciousness.

Make a list of at least twenty things in your life that you might consider blessings. For example:

- I live in an area that has very little crime and where my neighbors know and like me.

- Judy has been very generous with me, lending me equipment so I don't always have to buy it.

- I sleep well at night.

- I have a great massage therapist.

Make a list of twenty positive things about your child-hood. Make at least half of these about your mother. For example:

- My brother protected me at school when I was little.

- My mother took me for medical care when I needed it and was proactive around my headaches.

- My father introduced us to wild areas in nature.

- We used to sing in the car on road trips, and this was enjoyable.

- My mother cared about how I looked without being too controlling about it.

If you keep these lists available for reference, then, when a sense of deprivation starts setting in, you have something to use to counteract it.

### General tonics

There are some things that are just plain healing, regardless of the particular deficit or injury. They are "general tonics" that strengthen the system, including things like creativity and self-expression, cultivating a friendly relationship with your body, nurturing self-talk, and time spent in nature. Many have found in Mother Nature the holding that was missing for them earlier.

Pay attention to what is "good medicine" for you. Just as the Good Mother stays attuned to the needs of her child, your job is to stay attuned to your needs and provide the things that are nourishing and strengthening.

In this chapter I've encouraged you to take responsibility for meeting some of the deficits of your childhood. In combination with the preceding four chapters, it gives you enough material to work with for a long time. Enough to change your whole experience, transforming your story.

# 12.

# Changing the Story

The term *story* can be used in a couple of different ways. One is to refer to our account of something, the story we tell ourselves about it. This story that we tell ourselves may be very different from the objective facts and often makes it hard to see the objective facts. Caught in a deprivation story, for example, we fail to see how much we do have what we need.

The word *story* can also be used to refer to a more objective account of events, as when we think about someone's life narrative. Here we are looking at the sequence of events that compose that life.

In this chapter we'll look at our mother's story (second meaning) and see how that impacts our story (first meaning). We'll see how these influences pass along to the next generation. We'll also consider what all of this reparative work means for our actual relationships with our mothers now, as adults, and the ongoing nature of healing.

## Your mother's story

Our own subjective story, maintained by our childhood feelings, is by nature, self-centered. We interpret the world according to our experience. We know Mother by who she is to us.

When we stop there—who she was and still is to us—we miss a big piece. If you are a parent, can you imagine being known only through your interactions with one of your children? There are so many more aspects to you, so many other parts of your life that deeply influence who you are as a parent.

A large part of healing is stepping out of the limited story we replay about our mother and actually letting her emerge as a person. We need to see her life as it was. This exercise may help.

---

**Telling your mother's story (an exercise)**

There are several ways you can do this exercise. One would be to ask a friend to listen as you tell your mother's life story. Another option is to write it on paper. You can do this in any length and detail that you want. You can do this without the aid of the questions below, or you can use them as a prompt. Not every question may be relevant or something you can answer.

- What do you know about your mother's childhood, including family circumstances? Was she close to her parents? How many siblings did she have, and where was she in the lineup?

- Was her childhood happy? How do you think she experienced it?

- What seemed important to her as she emerged into young adulthood? What did she want out of life?

- How much do you think she had "found herself" before starting a family?

- How did she negotiate intimate relationships?

- Why did she have children?

o  What was it like for her to be a mother of young children? What about this might be particularly hard for her? What kind of support did she have?

o  What else was going on at the time? What was happening in the household and in the world? What social and economic stresses were present?

o  What do you know about her health and overall energy level?

o  What were the circumstances of your birth? How may these circumstances have affected your bonding with your mother?

o  If she worked outside the home, what was her job like? Did she enjoy it? Was she empowered there?

o  How was it for her to be a parent of adolescents?

o  Was there a childhood age or stage that seemed hardest for her to show up as a parent? What do you relate this to?

o  What other events in her young and middle adulthood were important?

o  What were her greatest assets? Her greatest deficits?

o  What do you think were the biggest struggles in her life?

o  Do you think she felt satisfied with how she parented you?

o  What aspects of her life were most unfulfilled?

o  What regrets might she have, if she could be totally honest?

o  Now think of a title for her life story. What would capture the essence of it?

### The stepping-stones of your mother's life (an exercise)

Here is an alternative (or supplemental) way to paint your mother's story with broad brushstrokes. It is based on a journaling technique developed by Ira Progoff, inventor of the Intensive Journal, and is called a stepping-stone list. Progoff used the term *stepping-stones* to refer to major life markers, although they are not always events per se. An item on a stepping stone list could refer to a whole period of life that has a certain atmosphere or quality to it.

Progoff suggests limiting stepping-stone lists to eight or ten items and never more than twelve. It is not necessary to put them in chronological order or even order of importance. Creating a stepping-stone list is simply a process of letting these markers come to mind and writing them down. A quiet, receptive state can facilitate this more easily than thinking too hard.

With this instruction in mind, make a list of eight to twelve significant markers in your mother's life.

### A letter from Mother (an exercise)

Here is a third exercise that might be revealing. Write a letter to yourself from your mother. It doesn't matter if your mother is alive or has passed on, or even if you are still in touch with her. Imagine what she might say to you if she were able to be genuinely disclosing. The letter may be about your relationship, a problem, what she wants for you . . . anything that comes to mind as perhaps unsaid. Note after this exercise how you feel.

There are also therapeutic techniques for taking Mother's perspective. In Gestalt therapy, role-playing, Psychodrama, and Family Constellation work, you or another might take Mother's perspective, speaking and acting as her, although sometimes from a deeper soul perspective than the persona shown to the world. In one of these stand-in experiences, a "mother" disclosed that she was empty and had nothing to give. It was painful for her to look at her daughter because she recognized her daughter had needed more.

Understanding Mother's experience is important. It helps us not personalize it so much, for one thing. We can more easily slip out of feeling unlovable, for example, when we see that Mother had limitations in expressing love. Rather than simply feeling lost and unshepherded, you can see that Mother had absolutely no experience guiding anyone, and probably had received no guidance herself.

The more we see our mothers clearly, the easier it is to find some compassion for them. They really were doing the best they could.

### Your story

"Developing compassion for the wounded mother does not preclude honoring the pain of the hurt child within oneself," writes therapist and author Evelyn Bassoff.[82] Mother's story is just part of the picture. There's also our story of what we've been through.

As I mentioned in the last chapter, our story is not always fully conscious, although we can make it conscious. Just as I invited you in the first exercise of the chapter to tell your mother's story, I invite you now to tell your story, either aloud to another or on paper. It can be the long or the short version. An advantage of the abbreviated version is that it's often easier to see the themes. What stands out when you consider your entire life experience?

When I first worked with my story, it was too hard for me to begin in childhood. It was too captivating, too tragic, too sad, and I found it hard to move on from there. I decided to start from the point of leaving home at age eighteen and to continue the story past the present time into the future, and that story made me smile. I liked the ending, and I could feel my empowerment and healing. I think now I could go back and start it in childhood, stating the truth of it but no longer so snared by the feelings that they overshadow everything else.

As you heal, your story changes. As you more objectively understand why your mother failed in the ways she did and take responsibility for mothering yourself, meeting your needs, and finding the mothering you need, you change your life.

## The dance between you

The intersection of the two stories, your mother's and your own, creates the dance between you. This is very important to keep in mind and helps explain how our siblings can have experiences so different from our own. Siblings come in with different sensitivities, have different needs, and are a different match with Mother. The hardier the baby and the closer the match, the easier it goes, all else being equal. But all else is not equal. For example, a child who is the tender age of twelve months will experience Mother grieving the loss of a parent or spouse differently than a child who is six. So the dance between each child and mother is unique.

> ‣ What adjectives describe your relationship with your mother? Is it cool? Adversarial? Have there been particular points of conflict? Is it perhaps superficial and obligatory? Are there points in the dance where there is closeness? If so, how do you feel at such moments? Do you like the closeness, or is it uncomfortable in some way and hard to fully accept?

We used stepping-stones when looking at Mother's life. Now let's make a list of stepping-stones for your relationship with her. Limiting your list to eight to twelve items, note the major markers in this relationship.

## How do I not pass this along to my children?

Many have recognized that what we haven't healed, we repeat, but when we have healed from a pattern we experienced in our families (even a pattern with a long history), we can break that pattern and do it differently for the next generation.

Harville Hendrix and Helen Hunt, in their parenting guide *Giving the Love That Heals,* assert that parents wound their children in the same stage of development as they were wounded. Their approach revolves around healing childhood wounds in the container of a conscious marriage, but that's just one way. They also believe that parents heal themselves when they are able to stretch and give their children what they didn't get themselves.[83]

I saw both of these phenomena in the people I interviewed. It was clear that many patterns relating both to parenting and to marriage were cross-generational. There were also numerous examples of patterns changing when people really worked at it. One woman talked about how hard she worked to parent in a different way than her mother did. She found that becoming a mother and working so diligently at it had helped her fill the hole left by her mother.

Laurie had a different story. Rather than filling the hole left by Mother, having her first child further exposed the hole. Experiencing an outpouring of what could only be called maternal instinct, she could not fathom how any woman could give birth and not feel this. This led to Laurie confronting her mother and demanding an explanation for her emotional absence.

A few of those I interviewed said that their parents had evolved over time without obvious intervention and were good grandparents. I suspect these are cases where there were specific stresses that interfered with their parenting or where they matured through some process of growth. Others became totally disengaged, under-responsive grandparents, just as they had been under-responsive, disengaged parents. We can't count on the mere passage of time to make the changes we want to see.

The most important things you can do to change the family legacy are to educate yourself about parenting and to do your own healing work.

## What about Mother?

A hornet's nest for many undermothered adults is how to relate to Mother now, if she's still alive. There isn't one answer that is going to work for everyone. Some people find the best option is to have no contact with their mothers or only very limited contact. It is often hard for people to give themselves this option, but sometimes we can reasonably expect no improvement and need to protect ourselves from behavior that brings nothing but pain. Outside of this, the major question for most of the undermothered is whether to try to improve their current relationship and how much to invest.

It may be shocking to consider that your current relationship with your mother can be quite separate from the journey you take to heal your mother wounds. Of course your healing will affect the relationship, if only by affecting your feelings and responses—which is no small thing. Yet in the end, it's a two-person dance, and your mother has her part, too. Mothers who are very shut down are likely to remain that way. Their capacity to change their moves may be very limited.

So you may discover and grieve the Original Loss, may fill the holes or get re-parented, and your actual mother may never be part of this journey or even consciously know about it. You can decide to share your disappointments, your struggle, or your successes with her, but she may not be able to participate much. In "No place to go for help" (p. 103), I described mothers who were unable to respond to their adult child's needs, even when the needs were great. Sharing brings no guarantee of being met. Sometimes Mom doesn't want more contact.

It is also possible that she may be open to a closer relationship. In those I spoke with whose relationship with their mothers improved, I noticed that it was generally the grown child who initiated the changes. It seemed to come with the adult child's capacity to extend warmth to the mother who, for the most part, had failed to extend warmth to her child. It came as these healed adult children were able to understand Mother's limitations, forgive, and want to include Mother in their lives.

Several of these offspring had also confronted their mothers. Clearing the air had served a purpose, perhaps then allowing greater warmth to flow between them. Confronting is an act of engagement and an act of intimacy if done right.

A mother can, of course, initiate more closeness with an adult child, and an adult child can be the hesitant one. One woman told me that when her mother ended a phone call with a totally unfamiliar "Love ya," it was so out of place that she couldn't respond. She also had fears of her mother's engulfment, even though the mother had been experienced as quite absent and disengaged. These issues are complex; even in a very chilly relationship you can feel a lack of boundaries.

It's important to ask yourself what you want, to assess what is possible as objectively as possible, and to know what kind of risks you are willing to take. Here are some questions that may help you.

> What do you think is your mother's capacity to have a warmer, more genuine relationship?

> What is your capacity for this with her?

➤ What do you want? Do you have some *shoulds*
operating—for instance, that you should be close to
your mother? What if you set these aside for a moment?

➤ If things never improve, how would that be?

➤ Are there fears you have about the relationship
becoming more real?

➤ If she sometimes responds to your overtures and at
other times does not, how would that be for you?

## Holding your process/holding your self

If you've been working this process, if you are on this journey of
healing, you know that it is very hard work. It is major recon-
struction. We are reworking ourselves on so many levels from
the hardwiring of the limbic brain to our core beliefs, from our
self-concept to how we relate to others, from the anxiety in
our chest to our ability to love, make money, and get a good
night's sleep.

Most likely this process will take several years if not into
the decades. I hesitate to say this out of concern that you'll find
that discouraging. But you may also be discouraged if you think
this is going to be a quick process, and it's not. No one I know
who has worked through this wound has done so quickly.

It is thus important to pace yourself, to take breaks, to be
able to see your progress and take pride in that. You don't want
to mimic the mother who never saw your accomplishments,
let alone celebrate them.

The process of growth is not a straight line but a spiral.
You'll cycle through similar issues many times. If you experience each cycle without change, that's a signal to get more
help, but otherwise expect to need to lament what was missing, grieve the injustices, and fulfill the unmet needs multiple
times. It won't be forever. There is grace in the healing process,
so although it's not like one good cry can make up for years of

repressed sadness, it can take you further down the field than you might think.

A Good Mommy understands that the process of growth is uneven and doesn't shame or scold her child for falling back at times. It is important to have that kind of compassion and patience with ourselves. We're doing the best we can, and some days are simply harder than others.

If you would like to join a discussion list to share your journey, the ups and downs, the ache of unmet needs, the embarrassment, the healing victories, you can sign up at www. jasmincori.com. Sorry, this first list is for women only. If you're male and would like to moderate a similar list, please contact me at my Web site, and I'll help in ways that I can. The list is for those of you whose mothers were emotionally absent and who are working to heal this wound, to know that you are not alone.

### Does healing ever end?

Although the process of healing never really ends, the hurt may, and the feeling of being a motherless child may disappear completely. The reason healing doesn't end is that we're always changing. Even just the simple passage of time changes our perspective, once we have become unglued from the past. So how we feel the first year or two after the bulk of our healing has occurred will be different than ten years later, when the past feels even further away.

When there has been significant injury, it's never as if that didn't happen. There is always at least the memory of the wound, if not some remaining sensitivity. But the power of that wound diminishes with healing, and our response to any poking in that area changes. Rather than get caught in childhood feelings that are triggered, we can learn to turn our attention slightly and ask the child inside what it needs now. We can *respond* to the feelings rather than stay trapped in them.

As we work through these wounds, our identity slowly changes. After all, our story has changed. Our life has changed. And it's time for the internal narrative to change as well. As one interviewee told me, "There's still a wound, but it doesn't run my life. It doesn't define who I am."

For those who are able to receive the care of someone standing in for the Good Mother or who are able to become that Good Mother to their own inner child, the feeling of being unmothered can be replaced by a feeling of being well mothered. You can feel loved, supported, and cared for. No, you can't go back and relive the past, but you can have now what you deserved to have then. As novelist Tom Robbins said, "It's never too late to have a happy childhood."

Appendix

# Be Kind to Yourself: Practicing Good Self-Care During Times of Emotional Healing

Many people have no sense of what it means to take care of themselves. Adults with emotionally absent mothers don't have a model of what attuned, attentive care looks like and have often learned to override distress signals. A client with this history looked at me a little blankly and asked, "What is self-care? I don't really know what that means. Eating well, and sleeping and exercising?"

Yes, and so much more.

- 🍃 Good self-care is finding things that feel good to your heart, whether a favorite stone, a song, sitting somewhere special, calling someone special.

- 🍃 Good self-care is not pushing yourself to function at your optimal level when you're going through a rough patch.

- 🍃 Good self-care is holding with compassion the person who is suffering and has suffered so much. In this case that person is you. Can you have as much compassion for yourself as you would have for your best friend going through what you're going through?

- 🍃 Good self-care is finding (healthy) activities that give you a moment of pleasure or are a time out from what is so stressful.

🍂 Good self-care is being kind to yourself. Can you speak to yourself with as much empathy and caring as you would to a loved one? Can you touch your face or your arm with tenderness? Can you give yourself a break when you need one?

🍂 Good self-care is being responsive to your needs rather than shutting out anything that is painful or inconvenient and gets in the way of functioning. Your feelings and needs are important and deserve to be attended to with respect and loving care.

Caring for someone recovering from an illness often means bringing food and helping out, so the person can rest and heal. In a similar way, caring for yourself when recovering from emotional pain means supplying nourishment and doing what you can to make your life easier. It means that *you*—your well-being—comes first and is more important than keeping up with expectations. It's nice to keep up as best you can, but it's not as important as your healing process.

Just as you might protect an injured finger with padding, good self-care provides a cushion to your nervous system. It is paying attention to all those things that affect you: sound, temperature, light, the effect of different food and drink on your digestive system, the effect of various people on your emotional system. When we are healing emotional wounds, our nervous system is doing extra work and starts with the disadvantage of already being compromised.

Knowing this, you allow yourself a little more "margin" than usual: an extra hour in bed, time to journal when you would have been paying bills, the option to leave the obligatory social gathering (or not go) because you just want to be alone.

You have feedback in this process. When you feel your body relax or you have a little more space emotionally, your self-care is working. Keep it up!

# Notes

1. Robert Karen, PhD, *Becoming Attached: First Relationships and How They Shape Our Capacity to Love* (New York: Oxford University Press, 1998), p. 230.
2. David J. Wallin, *Attachment in Psychotherapy* (New York: Guilford, 2007), n. 1, p. 24.
3. Diana Fosha, *The Transforming Power of Affect: A Model for Accelerated Change* (New York: Basic Books/Perseus Book Group, 2000), p. 64.
4. Ibid., p. 65.
5. Ibid.
6. Most of this list is my creation, although some are also noted in Jack Lee Rosenburg with Marjorie L. Rand and Diane Asay's book *Body, Self & Soul: Sustaining Integration* (Atlanta: Humanics, 1985), pp. 207–214. Also, Pamela Levin has affirmations similar to these for every developmental stage in her book *Cycles of Power: A User's Guide to the Seven Seasons of Life* (Deerfield Beach, FL: Health Communications Inc., 1988 and later self-published by the Nourishing Company). Her affirmations were first published in an earlier work, *Becoming the Way We Are: An Introduction to Personal Development In Recovery and In Life* (Berkeley, CA: self-published, 1974).
7. Harville Hendrix, PhD, and Helen Hunt, MA, MLA, *Giving the Love That Heals: A Guide for Parents* (New York: Pocket Books, 1997), p. 214.
8. Cesareans have been correlated with a mother–baby attachment gap. Mothers who give birth by C-section have been found to "take longer to begin to interact with their babies, have less positive reactions to them after birth, and interact less with them at home. In one study, a month after cesarean birth, the mothers had much less eye-to-eye contact with their babies." Susan Kuchinskas, "The Mother/Baby Attachment Gap," retrieved from www.hugthemonkey.com/2006/10/the_motherbaby_.html on April 25, 2008.
9. This is based on a study of maternal levels of oxytocin (sometimes called the love hormone) during pregnancy, which revealed that mothers with higher levels "gazed at their babies longer, touched their babies affectionately, had positive expressions while interacting with their baby, and reported checking on their baby more often than moms with lower oxytocin levels during pregnancy." Miranda Hiti, "Pregnancy Levels of the Hormone Oxytocin May Influence Mother–Child Bonding," *WebMD Medical News*, October, 16, 2007, retrieved from www.webmd.com/baby/news/20071016/hormone-may-help-baby-bond on April 25, 2008.
10. This is modified some with infants who have significant sensory and neurological issues that interfere with their ability to demonstrate

attachment behaviors. With the right intervention, these differences can be overcome and, once more, the mother's behaviors become key.

11. Allan Shore, reported in Sue Gerhardt, *Why Love Matters: How Affection Shapes a Baby's Brain* (New York: Brunner-Routledge, Taylor & Francis Group, 2004), p. 41.
12. Mario Mikulincer and Phillip R. Shaver, *Attachment in Adulthood: Structure, Dynamics, and Change* (New York: Guilford Press, 2007), p. 38.
13. Karen, *Becoming Attached*, p. 238.
14. Susan Anderson, *The Journey from Abandonment to Healing* (New York: Berkeley Books, 2000), pp. 77–78.
15. Daniel J. Siegel, "Toward an Interpersonal Neurobiology of the Developing Mind: Attachment Relationships, 'Mindsight,' and Neural Integration," *Infant Mental Health Journal* 22, no. 1: p. 77 (citing Cassidy and Shaver, 1999).
16. Wallin, *Attachment in Psychotherapy*, 22.
17. Ruth P. Newton, PhD, citing 2005 research by L. A. Sroufe, B. Egeland, E. Carlson, and W. A. Collins, in *The Attachment Connection: Parenting a Secure and Confident Child Using the Science of Attachment Theory* (Oakland, CA: New Harbinger Publications, 2008), 27.
18. Shirley Jean Schmidt, MA, LPC, citing Siegel, "Toward an Interpersonal Neurobiology," in *The Developmental Needs Meeting Strategy* (San Antonio: DNMS Institute, 2006), p. 17.
19. Siegel, "Toward an Interpersonal Neurobiology," p. 77.
20. Gerhardt, *Why Love Matters*, pp. 65–79.
21. The books detailing this tend to be quite technical. Authors to see include Allan Schore, PhD, and Daniel Siegel, MD. The most readable version of the research can be found in *Why Love Matters* by Sue Gerhardt.
22. Gerhardt, *Why Love Matters*, pp. 38, 44.
23. Studies of middle-class children show slightly lower rates of insecure attachment and hover around 30 percent, while all studies of American children come in at closer to 38 percent. Karen, *Becoming Attached*, pp. 220, 224.
24. Ibid., p. 329.
25. Ibid., pp. 156, 373, reporting on both Ainsworth and Main.
26. Gerhardt, *Why Love Matters*, 93.
27. Mary Main, reported in Karen, *Becoming Attached*, p. 224.
28. Fosha, *Transforming Power of Affect*, p. 52.
29. Black, *Mothering Without a Map*, (New York: Penguin Books, 2004), p. 64.
30. Karen, *Becoming Attached*, p. 387.
31. This was a pattern identified by attachment pioneer John Bowlby.
32. Malcolm L. West and Adrienne E. Sheldon-Keller, *Patterns of Relating: An Adult Attachment Perspective* (New York: Guilford, 1994), p. 75.
33. Newton, citing 1999 research by Belsky in *Attachment Connection*, p. 29.
34. Main and Hesse, 1990, cited in Siegel, "Toward an Interpersonal Neurobiology," p. 78, and also described in other places.
35. Newton, *Attachment Connection*, p. 30.

36. Siegel, "Toward an Interpersonal Neurobiology," p. 78.
37. Daniel J. Siegal, "Attachment and Self-Understanding: Parenting with the Brain in Mind," in *Attachment and Human Survival,* Marci Green and Marc Scholes, eds. (New York: Karnac, 2004), p. 34.
38. Joan Woodward, "Introduction to Attachment Theory" in *Attachment and Human Survival,* Marci Green and Marc Scholes, eds. (New York: Karnac, 2004), p. 16.
39. Newton, PhD, *Attachment Connection,* p. 30.
40. Ibid.
41. Siegal, "Attachment and Self-Understanding," p. 29.
42. Gerhardt, *Why Love Matters,* 147.
43. Fosha, *Transforming Power of Affect,* p. 54.
44. These items come from a variety of scales and descriptions, including a measure of adult attachment style developed by Hazan and Shaver (1987) found in Mikulincer and Shaver, *Attachment in Adulthood.*
45. Karen, *Becoming Attached,* p. 227.
46. Karen, *Becoming Attached,* p. 228.
47. As Diana Fosha reports, "Anxiety is a reaction to the nonavailability or nonresponsiveness of the caregiver and is rooted in the feeling of being alone in the face of psychic danger." *Transforming Power of Affect,* 47. Earlier in the same book is this support: "Just as the feeling of safety has its origins in a secure attachment relationship with an available and responsive caregiver (Bowlby, 1988; Sandler, 1960), similarly anxiety and the defense mechanisms to which . . . anxiety gives rise have *their* origins in an attachment relationship with an unavailable or unresponsive caregiver," pp. 39–40.
48. Michael St. Clair, *Object Relations and Self Psychology: An Introduction,* second edition (Pacific Grove, CA: Brooks/Cole Publishing, 1996), p. 79.
49. Ashley Montagu, *Touching: The Human Significance of the Skin,* third edition (New York: Harper Paperbacks, 1986), p. 126.
50. Karen, *Becoming Attached,* p. 340.
51. Karen, *Becoming Attached,* p. 339.
52. Daniel N. Stern, MD, *Diary of a Baby* (New York: HarperCollins/Basic Books, 1990), p. 61.
53. Black, *Mothering Without a Map,* p. 60.
54. Stern, *Diary of a Baby,* p. 62.
55. T. Berry Brazelton, MD, and Bertrand G. Cramer, MD, *The Earliest Relationship: Parents, Infants, and the Drama of Early Attachment* (Reading, MA: Addison-Wesley/A Merloyd Lawrence Book, 1990), p. 109.
56. Gerhardt, *Why Love Matters,* p. 124 (citing research).
57. Gerhardt, *Why Love Matters,* p. 21.
58. Brazelton and Cramer, *The Earliest Relationship,* 110.
59. I do not work in the field of early intervention, where there may be some exceptions. In cases where the baby has a neurological or sensory disorder, mother and baby often need interventions to help the baby attach.
60. Judith Viorst, *Necessary Losses: The Loves, Illusions, Dependencies and Impossible Expectations That All of Us Have to Give Up in Order to Grow* (New York: Simon & Schuster, 1986), p. 32.

61. Ibid., p. 29.

62. Fosha, *Transforming Power of Affect,* pp. 54–55.

63. Rose-Emily Rothenberg, "The Orphan Archetype," in *Reclaiming the Inner Child,* Jeremiah Abrams, ed. (Los Angeles: Tarcher, 1990), p. 92.

64. John Bradshaw, *Homecoming: Reclaiming and Championing Your Inner Child* (New York: Bantam, 1990), p. 75.

65. Ibid., p. 78.

66. Edward Z. Tronick, "Dyadically Expanded States of Consciousness and the Process of Therapeutic Change," *Infant Mental Health Journal* 19, no. 3 (1998): pp. 290–299.

67. "Donald Winnicott," retrieved from http://en.wikipedia.org/wiki/Donald_Winnicott on April 12, 2008.

68. Wallin, *Attachment in Psychotherapy,* p. 121.

69. Wallin, *Attachment in Psychotherapy,* p. 119.

70. Soonja Kim, "Sweet Re-Mothering for Undermothered Women," first published in *Open Exchange Magazine* and retrieved from the author's Web site, www.motheringundermotheredwomen.com on March 4, 2010.

71. Ibid.

72. Ibid.

73. Dennis L. Merritt, PhD, "Brief Psychotherapy: A Jungian Approach," retrieved from www.dennismerrittjungiananalyst.com/Brief_Psychotherapy.htm on June 24, 2008.

74. Anderson, *Journey from Abandonment,* p. 76.

75. I believe Freud used this; certainly his student Theodore Reik did. Also the poets William Wordsworth and Gerard Manley Hopkins did in the 1800s, and it has more recently been used as the title of a song, an album, and even a TV episode.

76. Nancy J. Napier, *Recreating Your Self: Help for Adult Children of Dysfunctional Families* (New York: W. W. Norton, 1990), p. 151.

77. Jean Illsley Clarke and Connie Dawson, *Growing Up Again: Parenting Ourselves, Parenting Our Children* (Center City, MN: Hazeldon, 1999), p. 8.

78. Bradshaw, *Homecoming,* p. 71.

79. Bradshaw, *Homecoming,* p. 72.

80. Gerhardt, *Why Love Matters,* p. 26.

81. Jett Psaris, PhD, and Marlena S. Lyons, PhD, *Undefended Love* (Oakland, CA: New Harbinger, 2000), p. 141.

82. Evelyn Silton Bassoff, PhD, *Mothering Ourselves: Help and Healing for Adult Daughters* (New York: Dutton/Penguin Group, 1991), p. 175.

83. Hendrix and Hunt, *Giving the Love That Heals,* p. 6.

# Resources

## HEALING MOTHER WOUNDS

**Online Support Group (for women)**
Information about this group can be found at www.jasmincori.com
by following the links for The Emotionally Absent Mother and then for
the support group.

*Mothering Ourselves: Help and Healing for Adult Daughters*
Evelyn Silten Bassoff, PhD (New York: Dutton/Penguin Group, 1991)
A book for undermothered women by a compassionate psychotherapist. Includes stories of emotional neglect and undermothering, myths,
and guidance on healing. Primary theme is becoming your own good
mother. Highly recommended.

*Warming the Stone Child: Myths and Stories About Abandonment*
*and the Unmothered Child*
Clarissa Pinkola Estés, PhD (Louisville, CO: Sounds True [audiotape],
1990)
Jungian therapist, bestselling author, and poet Dr. Estés is a skilled
storyteller, and many will find this tape enchanting. Focuses on the
unmothered child's need for guidance.

*In Her Image: The Unhealed Daughter's Search for Her Mother*
Kathie Carlson (Boston: Shambhala, 1989)
The author is a Jungian therapist who considers this issue from the
perspective of Jungian and transpersonal psychology, feminism, and
developmental psychology.

*When You and Your Mother Can't Be Friends: Resolving the Most*
*Complicated Relationship of Your Life*
Victoria Secunda (Concord CA: Delta, 1991)
For daughters only, this book provides advice on how to come to terms
with or improve your relationship with an abusive mother.

*I Am My Mother's Daughter: Making Peace With Mom—Before It's*
*Too Late*
Iris Krasnow (New York: Perseus Books Group, 2006)
Another book focusing on adult daughters repairing the bond with
Mother; includes a large number of interviews.

Note: There are also books specific to various kinds of mothers, such
as narcissistic mothers, borderline mothers, and abusive mothers; I
have not included these here.

## FOR PARENTS

*Mothering Without a Map*
Kathryn Black (New York: Penguin Books, 2000)
An excellent book for women who were undermothered and who are or are contemplating becoming mothers. A Yahoo! discussion group is available: http://groups.yahoo.com/group/mothering_without_a_map.

*Growing Up Again: Parenting Ourselves, Parenting Our Children*
Jean Illsley Clarke and Connie Dawson (Center City, MN: Hazelden, 1998)
This is a relatively short self-help book written in a simple, direct style. Helpful to parents who were underparented.

*Parenting from the Inside Out: How a Deeper Self-Understanding Can Help You Raise Children Who Thrive*
Daniel Siegel, MD, and Mary Hartzel, MEd. (New York: Tarcher, 2004)
Some will find the research threaded throughout a little more technical than meets their needs. Dr. Siegel is an authority on brain research related to attachment.

*Zero to Three: National Center for Infants, Toddlers and Families*
The mission of this nonprofit is to translate research findings about experiences that help children thrive into a range of practical tools and resources. www.zerotothree.org.

## INNER CHILD

*Recovery of Your Inner Child*
Lucia Capacchione, PhD (New York: Simon & Schuster, 1991)
Practical, enchanting, and heartwarming, this guide will help you work with your inner child. Includes over forty exercises.

*Reclaiming the Inner Child*
Edited by Jeremiah Abrams (New York: Tarcher, 1990)
This anthology offers a span of perspectives from well-known authors and clinicians on inner child and orphan archetypes and the healing process.

*Homecoming: Reclaiming and Healing Your Inner Child*
John Bradshaw (New York: Bantam, 1992)
A guide to working with the wounded inner child. Along with a general description of the process, includes developmental stages and the needs in each. Bradshaw also has videos and audio books; you can easily find these online.

## ATTACHMENT & RELATIONSHIP

Unfortunately, most of the books about attachment are too technical to be of interest to the average reader. In this list, I focus on resources that are more useful to the layperson.

### Hold Me Tight: Seven Conversations for a Lifetime of Love
Sue Johnson (Little, Brown and Company, 2008)
Sue Johnson is the developer of Emotionally Focused Couples Therapy. This guide, an adjunct to therapy (or perhaps replacement), teaches couples how to sort through the usual conflicts that happen in partnerships and identify the attachment needs underneath.

### Getting the Love You Want: A Guide for Couples
Harville Hendrix (New York: Holt Paperbacks, 2007)
Hendrix is one of two founders of Imago Relationship Therapy. Covers the Unconscious Marriage, where unmet childhood needs interfere with the current relationship, and the Conscious Marriage, which fulfills those childhood needs in a positive manner.

### The Journey from Abandonment to Healing
Susan Anderson, CSW (New York: Berkeley Books, 2000)
An insightful book about how our need for attachment informs our intimate relationships and the painful process that occurs when such relationships fail and the abandonment wound is stimulated.

### Becoming Attached: First Relations and How They Shape Our Capacity to Love
Robert Karen, PhD (New York: Oxford University Press, 1998)
An engaging, well-written book detailing the history of attachment research and ideas. More for professionals.

### Why Love Matters: How Affection Shapes a Baby's Brain
Sue Gerhardt (New York: Brunner-Routledge, 2004)
This book makes accessible the latest findings in the neuroscience of attachment. Highly recommended.

### The Attachment Connection: Parenting a Secure and Confident Child Using the Science of Attachment Theory
Ruth P. Newton, PhD (Oakland, CA: New Harbinger Publications, 2008)
The purpose of this book is to bring attachment and affect regulation theories to parents and child care staff. The neurobiology is likely more complex than the average reader will find helpful.

You can take attachment-related tests online at www.yourpersonality. net, where you'll also find a summary of recent research.

# Acknowledgments

Every book, like every child, needs a good home. My deepest appreciation to Matthew Lore and The Experiment for providing such a welcoming home and such expert care.

I have been honored over the years to have a great many people share their inner lives with me, including the joys and disappointments of their childhood. Thank you to clients, students, and friends who have shared their stories with me and to those who generously gave their time to be interviewed for this book. May your suffering and your hard-earned lessons enrich the lives of others on this journey. Thank you to the therapists who shared their impressions and expertise and the early readers who offered valuable feedback.

There are also a few individuals I will call out by name. First, special thanks to Sara Lynn Swift, who combed through the manuscript, offering important insights. Willow Arlenea, wise woman and coauthor of *The Tarot of Transformation*, also provided valuable feedback and has been a wonderful support. Thank you to Raji Raman, my unpaid editor, for her labor of love; Betsy Kabrick for her insights and contribution; Salila Shen for her assistance with the partner section; and Amber Vallotton for helping with the online support group. Finally, deep gratitude to my therapist, Konstanze Hacker, who, through her gentleness and caring, provided me with an experience of the Good Mother, encouraged the sweet child within me to develop and emerge, and so patiently and capably shepherded me through the process of healing.

# Index

# About the Author

**JASMIN LEE CORI, MS, LPC,** is a licensed psychotherapist in private practice in Boulder, Colorado, whose specialty is working with adults who experienced childhood abuse and/or neglect.

An experienced educator, Jasmin taught over a dozen different psychology courses in a variety of colleges and professional schools, including training therapists in counseling skills. She has also worked in human service agencies.

Jasmin is the author of *Healing from Trauma: A Survivor's Guide to Understanding Your Symptoms and Reclaiming Your Life* (2008), *The Tao of Contemplation: Re-Sourcing the Inner Life* (2000), *The Tarot of Transformation* (with Willow Arlenea; 2002), and numerous articles, as well as a book of mystical poetry. She enjoys hiking, expressive movement groups, Sufi dancing, communing with nature and Spirit, and creativity and play with friends. For more information, visit www.jasmincori.com.